A Child of Destiny

A Child of Destiny
An Autobiography

K. Ramakrishna Rao

GITAM
(Deemed to be University)

PRINTWORLD
Publishers of Indian Traditions

Cataloging in Publication Data — DK
[Courtesy: D.K. Agencies (P) Ltd. <docinfo@dkagencies.com>]

Rao, K. Ramakrishna, author.

A child of destiny : an autobiography/K. Ramakrishna Rao.
pages cm
Includes bibliographical references.
ISBN 9788124610305 (Hb)

1. Rao, K. Ramakrishna. 2. Philosophers – India – Andhra Pradesh – Biography. 3. Psychologists – India – Andhra Pradesh – Biography. 4. Educators – India – Andhra Pradesh – Biography. I. Title.

LCC B5134.R36A3 2020 | DDC 181.4 23

ISBN: 978-81-246-1030-5
First published in India in 2020

Published by:
GITAM
(Deemed to be University)
Rushikonda, Visakhapatnam – 530 045 (A.P.)
Phone: (0891) 284 0312; Fax: (0891) 279 0037
e-mail: director_sgs@gitam.edu
Web: www.gitam.edu

and

D.K. Printworld (P) Ltd.
Regd. Office: "Vedaśrī", F-395, Sudarshan Park
(ESI Hospital) Metro Station, New Delhi - 110015
Phones : (011) 2545 3975, 2546 6019
e-mail : indology@dkprintworld.com
Web : www.dkprintworld.com

Printed by: D.K. Printworld (P) Ltd., New Delhi

Contents

In the Memory of
My Loving Wife for Sixty-nine Years

Shrimati Koneru Sarojini Devi

ప్రేమతో, చాలా, నీ బావయ్య

Preface

THE BRIEF AUTOBIOGRAPHICAL account presented in this volume is an attempt to show the significance of circumstances in shaping one's destiny. Volition has an important role to play, but intentions are insufficient to determine the outcome. Wisdom consists in taking advantage of the circumstances to move the events in the desired direction. Volition is the driving force but needs guidance for an appropriate outcome. It is hoped that this brief autobiography is sufficiently illustrative of this.

I grew up in a rural setting, economically backward and socially uninspiring in some ways. Yet it had other advantages that could be exploited to realize one's true potential. Rural living has its own nobility; it instills unadulterated values without any sophisticated encumbrances, and can help to drive the inner spirit toward self-realization. A judicious rural–urban mix could be a boon for one to blossom and harvest full inherent potential and talent.

This exercise is a description of the play of destiny in my own life. This has several lessons for me, and I hope it has something to offer to others.

My tryst with destiny is in many ways memorable and satisfying. There were many who were instrumental in materializing these events. My family had been and continues to be an important source of support and even inspiration. My beloved wife for 69 years traveled with me all the way sharing the spring days as well as the chills of life. Now she left me blissfully and peacefully breathing her last in her sleep at 2.00 a.m. on 03 May 2019. She was though less abled during the last few years, she was a joy of my life; now I feel orphaned and lonely; but she would not have wanted me to get sick and tired. So, I go on with my life, even though I find my evenings uninspiring and lifeless. My children live continents apart, on the other side of the globe. With the communications revolution in place now, the physical distance matters very little. However, now that my wife was gone, my children want me to spend more time in the US. Used to an active life in Visakhapatnam, I hesitate to spend my time in semi-retirement. I am now in search of a golden mean.

I thank Dr. Rositta Joseph for copy-editing the manuscript of this book with her characteristic care.

It is not inappropriate to say how fortunate I am to have such wonderful people around me to help. Rafi is with me wherever and whenever I need him. I have excellent facilities in my office at GITAM as well as great help at my home. I acknowledge my grateful thanks to all of them, who continue to support me. Their loving service sustains me and keeps me going with undiminished energy and enthusiasm.

1

Growing Up in a Rural Community

Introduction

LIFE IS A FLOWING STREAM, not a still pond. Therefore, there is likely to be dry spells as well as floods, turbulences and troubled periods, frustrations, despair and depression, and also times of tasting success and enjoying periods of pleasure. However, the goal of life to be happy is realized only in a state of equanimity and tranquility. Equanimity is not simply experiencing a state of stillness but it consists in striking a healthy balance between positive and negative states. What have I learned from my own life and experience? How could one strike a balance between extreme emotions one faces, whether delight or depression, success or failure?

Perhaps, it is not usually the case; but I have dabbled in my academic endeavors in diverse fields from conducting experimental studies to exploring inner states, from studying pragmatism to understanding idealism as philosophies of life, and from the investigation of *yoga* and consciousness to Gandhi's thought and his concept of nonviolence as a tool of personal transformation as well as a vehicle of social action and conflict resolution. However, there is a method in this madness, a running thread that binds them all together. It is investigating the link between science and spirituality, between the mundane and the transcendental, and between the ego and the other.

I began my academic career with an interest in studying human nature. Under the guidance of my early *guru*, Prof. Saileswar Sen, I was led to study parapsychology as a possible bridge between science and spirituality, a link between Eastern philosophies and Western science. However, largely because of the influence of Dr. J.B. Rhine, as my professional career was unfolding, the study of and research in parapsychology became an end in itself; and consumed a major part of my academic activities. I published scores of research papers and a few books beginning with *Psi Cognition* (1957) to the more recent one, *The Elements of Parapsychology* (2017); edited the *Journal of Parapsychology* for nearly two decades, and was elected as the President of Parapsychological Association, an international society of professionals involved in parapsychology, at three different times, first in 1965. With all this intimate involvement in parapsychological work in different roles, why do I now feel not so fully satisfied with all that; and have tended more recently to drift away from it? The reason seems to be that my genuine roots are in the Indian tradition; and that my involvement in parapsychology was an unintended transplant of that interest in an alien soil. Therefore, my growth was somewhat stunted. This was perhaps due to what I might call the "Rhinean Spell." I see in it the hand of destiny, by which I mean the force of circumstances rather than a self-generated will.

After decades of intimate involvement in parapsychology, in its limited sense of experimentally investigating human abilities that seem to transcend the normal sensory-motor functions, I see in recent times the broader contours of my pursuits and the place of consciousness as an overarching principle that governs the normal as well as the paranormal phenomena we encounter in life. What we had been hoping to capture by psi research was merely a drop in the vast ocean of consciousness. Indian psychology is a discipline that postulates that the person, the subject of its study, is a mirror that reflects the rays of consciousness. With this broader perspective of science and spirituality, I now find a harmonious blend of my seemingly varied explorations.

Birth and Growth in a Rural Community

I was a country boy; not born with a silver spoon; but with a very healthy environment to grow. I have very fond memories of living and learning in my early years in a very rural setting; but with some unusual privileges. My mother came from some kind of an aristocratic family in a remote village, Ramannapalem in Krishna district. I was born in Ramannapalem, and spent a lot of time in that village, pampered in all possible ways, being the eldest child in a prominent family in the village. My maternal grandfather was the village head. He moved with *jamindar*s, some kind of royalty, who controlled the landholdings in villages. The village heads, called *munsiff*s, were responsible for collecting the land taxes from the villagers as well as looking after the local law and order matters. My maternal grandfather also used to mine for precious stones. In fact, we used to have quite a few of those at our home. I had a very enjoyable time in Ramannapalem with tons of freedom savoring the true flavor of rural life, little polluted by urbanization both in practices and thinking. I could pluck delicious fruits from the garden and relish eating them, hear the whispering of frogs in the well and the sweet songs of birds in the fields adjoining the house. I used to bathe and swim in a nearby flowing natural stream not too far from the place we lived. These are some of the sweetest memories of my early childhood I still cherish. Whatever I did in Ramannapalem was for fun. I fully relished rural life.

From my father's side, the story was somewhat different in that the family did not inherit an aristocratic tradition as in the case of my maternal grandparents. My paternal grandfather was also the village head. He had earned a reputation for his impeccable character and devotion to work. He was duly recognized and rewarded for his efforts to nail down a few notorious criminals. I recall, he had a baton with a sterling silver cap presented by the government in recognition of his meritorious work. I would have loved to inherit and keep it as a family heirloom. Alas! One of my father's younger brothers took it away and probably sold it for a pittance.

Even though the villages from where my father and mother came were nearly 50 miles apart, which in those days was a formidable distance, the marriage between my parents consummated, because my grandparents met each other frequently in Vijayawada (then called Bezwada) to deposit in the treasury their land revenue tax collections.

My father came from an agricultural family; however, their landholdings were too meager to support five brothers and two sisters. Therefore, he had to find other avenues for employment. So, he became a teacher in the village school, which later came under the jurisdiction of the district school system with the result he became a district employee with benefits of lifelong monthly pension after retirement. When his children grew up and financially well placed, he did not really need that small pension. However, he regularly collected and spent it to bring home some goodies to his grandchildren. My father's job as a teacher in the district school system was transferable to any other school in the district. However, he managed to stay almost throughout his career as a teacher in our ancestral village, because of the clout the family had with district administration. So, I did not move around, but spent most of my childhood in Enikepadu or Ramannapalem.

My father was a very docile, humble, and agreeable person. He highly valued education. He did everything he could to provide good education for his sons. Unfortunately, in those days little attention was given to girls. So, my sister, who is probably as bright, if not more than her brothers, did not have the benefit of higher education. If she had the same educational opportunities as her two brothers, I know, she would have excelled and possibly surpassed both of her brothers.

As mentioned, my maternal grandfather had in him a streak of aristocracy and royalty. He moved and interacted with *jamindar*s as we noted earlier. I was pampered, as I was the eldest child in the family; and was given the impression that I was superior to others. Such a superiority complex was a drawback. I became too self-assertive and indulgent, sometimes even aggressively so. This streak still haunts me a bit; and cautions me to exercise considerable restraint in my social interactions.

The families from my mother's and father's side, as we noted, were in such stark contrast. When my mother came to our ancestral home, where my father lived in Enikepadu, she came in a *meena*, a closed and decorated carriage carried by men. It was a spectacle not witnessed before in our village. My mother was never seen outside of her house. It was a big come down to live in the joint family set-up for one who was brought up in an aristocratic tradition. However, she never complained; and happily lived with my father who shared the joint family house with two of his other brothers. The house was large with a tiled roof, one of the impressive structures in the village abutting the main road between Bezwada and Eluru.

The recorded date of my birth is 4 October 1932. I have reason to think that it is the correct date because, even though my father came from a peasant family, he was a literate person, and a teacher who was meticulous in many ways, and clearly in maintaining records. He drafted legal documents to many illiterate peasants in the village. It is therefore most unlikely that he recorded a wrong date; and there was no reason, good or bad, that could have prompted him to enter a false date of my birth.

If 4 October is the day of my birth, it comes two days after M.K. Gandhi's. I consider this proximity quite significant because Mahatma Gandhi has been an inspiration for me since my school days. I recall how we sobbed for days when we listened to All India Radio news of his death on 30 January 1948. I was only 16 years old then; but the experience is still fresh and poignant.

Notwithstanding the many twists and turns in my professional activities, my interest in Gandhi has remained consistent and steady throughout my professional career. When I was engaged in parapsychological work, I was always reminded of Gandhi's "inner voice" episodes. In my studies of *yoga*, Gandhi's *yoga* of nonviolence stands out prominently. In my readings of consciousness, the notion of pure consciousness is strengthened by my familiarity with Gandhian thought and practices.

While Gandhi's ideas figure out so prominently in my intellectual pursuits, I fall far short in actually incorporating his practices into my own life and living. Gandhi had deservedly earned the reputation of being Mahatma. Mahatma's signal characteristic is that there is in him a harmonious blend of thought and action. Gandhi tried to translate his thoughts into practice, his principles and ideals into his daily deeds and conduct. He succeeded to a large extent in that difficult task. In my personal life, I must confess candidly, the cleavage between thought, passion, and action is unmistakably present.

In Enikepadu, there was less freedom of movement and greater discipline than in Ramannapalem. My father knew the value of education, and intended to give his children the best possible education. However, he was a member of a joint family living with his parents and two other brothers in the same house, as mentioned. This restricted what he could do. However, the joint family, situation provided me with an atmosphere of sharing and caring for each other. What was exciting in my childhood was the freedom I enjoyed in Ramannapalem; and what I did not relish so much were the restrictions in Enikepadu.

With all the respect I had for my father, who did everything possible to bring us up, give us a good education and make us settle in our lives, there were two things that I did not quite like. One, he used to inhale snuff, which I hated because it stood in the way of his outward cleanliness. Two, he used to play cards with cash bets, bordering on gambling. Sometimes, he used to borrow money from old women in the neighborhood paying significant interest. I really hated this streak in him. When I grew up and attended college bicycling every day from home, I became somewhat independent and defiant. I began joining my father's group to play cards with stakes. My father had no choice but stop playing; he could not digest that he would be playing cards with me among others for real stakes. So, it did the trick, as I hoped, he stopped playing cards for cash stakes.

To get back to my childhood story, I hated to come back to Enikepadu from my maternal grandparents' home, but I had no choice. In some ways, it helped me in the long run, because education at the elementary school in Ramannapalem was relatively poor compared to the one where my father taught. Further, my father was constantly watching my performance. Under his watchful eyes, I had a good foundation, which kept me well-grounded and prepared for future high school and college education.

After the fifth standard, there was no scope for further education in my village. My father was so strongly intent on providing me with further education that he looked around to find a place where he could send me for further education. His younger sister lived in a village called Mantena where there was a middle school. He sent me there to live with his sister's family and attend the school. It was possibly one of the worst years of my childhood. I hated the place.

We are a bit ahead of the story. When I was nine years old, my mother fell ill. In spite of everything my father and paternal grandparents could do to provide the best available medical care in Bezwada, she died, leaving behind two sons and a daughter. My father was relatively young; he could have married again. However, fearing that his next wife might neglect and ill-treat his children, he gave up any idea of remarrying. It was a big sacrifice. He gave up personal comforts to take care of his children. Myself and my sister were looked after by my paternal grandmother. My brother went to stay with my mother's sister in a village near Nuzvid in Krishna district. She had no children of her own. Brother attended the high school in Nuzvid going daily there from Annavaram, 2 miles away.

From Mantena, I moved to another village Edupugallu to attend the middle school. After one year there, I was sent to live with another cousin sister of my father in Kolavennu so that I could attend the high school at Punadipadu. This changed the course of my life as we would note.

The middle school in Edupugallu used to attract students from several nearby villages. In fact, students from Penamaluru about 3 miles away used to attend the school in Edupugallu. I vividly recall the mother of Ashok Atluri and Rupa used to bicycle from Penamaluru. It was somewhat unusual for girls to ride a bicycle in those days. She married one of my very close friends Dr. Shivaji. Unfortunately, she died in a fire accident in a marriage *pandal.*

Kolavennu is about 2 miles away from Punadipadu, where there is a high school. I used to walk this distance; there were no school buses. After an year or so, father bought me a new Hercules bicycle, which I enjoyed riding to the school; it was indeed a luxury for a middle-class family. During those days, there was no electricity in Kolavennu. We used to read under the light of kerosene lamps. I did my home work very quickly, and was early to go to bed. My aunt and uncle to whom I was entrusted, I knew, were a little worried, because other kids in the neighborhood used to study until late in the night. As it happened, several nephews of my uncle flunked the final exams in the high school; not only did I pass but secured a fairly high rank. This impressed my uncle very much.

After graduating from the high school, I joined the SRR & CVR College on the outskirts of Bezwada. It was not too far from my village; I could go by my bicycle without much strain. Between the college and our house, there was a village where my father's elder sister lived with her family. Returning from the college, I used to stop at their house and have a sumptuous meal. During the final year in the college, I lived along with some friends in a rented house near the college.

During the second year in college, I became very active, engaged in all kinds of pursuits, somewhat neglecting my studies. I became the secretary of the student wing of Congress Party. I had an office in Andhra Ratna Bhavan, and came to be very close to the President of AP Congress, Prof. N.G. Ranga, Vice-President Timma Reddy, and the Secretary Kandula Obul Reddy. We used to eat lunch together. A good stage was set for me to have a career in politics; and I was preparing for it. I relished involvement in public life. It was emotionally satisfying and personally challenging.

Marriage and College Years

Then, there was the game changer. My uncle in Kolavennu, impressed with my school record and sensing the potential for my future academic development in me, proposed the marriage of his eldest daughter to me. My father was thrilled because they were more affluent and financially better off than him. He agreed to our marriage without consulting me. When I learnt this, I was furious and emphatically said no. Father sobbed inconsolably; and said that he did everything to bring me up under great odds and that I now refuse to listen to him. He offered some kind of a *satyagraha* and left me with little choice. I was hooked; all my political ambitions evaporated. I married Sarojini on 5 May 1950.

Since I was involved in all kinds of non-academic work during my final year in college, I could not secure a high rank. Further, my elective subjects in college were Physics, Chemistry and Logic, a peculiar combination. At that time, SRR & CVR College did not offer biological sciences as electives. With this odd combination of Physics, Chemistry and Logic, I could not seek admission in engineering or medicine, the preferred professional avenues. I did not quite know what to do; and had little guidance from my elders. So, I joined the Hindu College in Machilipatnam to pursue BA in economics.

Tata Rao, one of my roommates in Vijayawada, joined BCom (Hons) at Andhra University in Waltair, Visakhapatnam. I was in regular contact with him.

He attended my marriage also. Tata Rao suggested that I go to Waltair and explore joining one of the courses, possibly geology which did not require mathematics as a prerequisite. So, I traveled to Waltair and met the Head of the Geology Department, Prof. C. Mahadevan. He seemed to like me, took me to the Principal Prof. Rangadhama Rao, Professor of Physics, and recommended that I might be admitted into BSc (Hons) course in geology. The principal received us warmly and looked at my curriculum vitae. He said he would like to help, but without the needed background in mathematics, I would not be able to do my physics at this level, which was a compulsory subsidiary subject for geology students. Therefore, it was in my interest, he said, I should not pursue this line of study.

Prof. Mahadevan shook his head, turned to me and said that he would like to help me; but there was very little he could do. However, he felt that the best course to pursue for me was philosophy and that I could specialize in psychology and prepare myself to appear for competitive examinations and hopefully join the Indian Administrative Service. He thought that I had the necessary personality and good physical appearance to be competitive in the national selection process. Prof. Mahadevan showed some kind of paternal interest in me. I was deeply moved by his gesture to help me, and strongly felt that I should follow his advice. I assured him that I would abide by his guidance. He drove me in his rickety old car to the office of Prof. Saileswar Sen, Head of the

Philosophy Department. Prof. Mahadevan told Prof. Sen, "I brought here my boy; you admit him in BA (Hons) philosophy course and take care of him." That was how I joined the Philosophy Department at Andhra University, where I had a long and satisfying innings. Let us note that Andhra University under the leadership of such stalwarts as C.R. Reddy and S. Radhakrishnan brought to the university eminent scholars and scientists without regard to their place of origin. Prof. Sen was from Bengal and Prof. Mahadevan was from what is now Tamil Nadu.

Prof. Sen heartily welcomed me. In those days, philosophy did not attract many students. Further, my academic credentials far exceeded those who normally joined the Philosophy Department. Prof. Sen and I bonded so well that he took me to his home several times. In fact, he showered more affection on me than on his own children. His daughter at the time was a doctoral fellow in the Department of English. She was justly jealous of how I was treated by her father, as she confessed to me later.

After joining the faculty, when I told Prof. Sen that I was bringing my wife to live with me in Waltair, he personally visited the house I was planning to rent. Only after his approval, I moved into it. The relationship between us resembled in significant ways the legendary *guru–shishya* relationship of yester years we hear about. When Prof. Sen was seriously ill and undergoing treatment at the King George Hospital in Visakhapatnam, he asked me to be with him at his bed side. As it happened, I was with him when he breathed his last.

K. Satchidananda Murty was then a lecturer in the Philosophy Department. He taught us logic and contemporary Western philosophy. A. Lakshmana Rao was our psychology teacher. The department offered specializations in Indian philosophy and educational and abnormal psychology. I chose the psychology route. I had Md. Ismail as a fellow student. We remained lifelong friends. His interest, however, was in Indian philosophy. He had good grounding in Telugu literature. He was closely associated with Devulapalli Krishna Sastry, a well-known lyric writer and poet. My close association with Md. Ismail led me to appreciate modern Telugu poetry. I even attempted to dabble myself in writing some poems. One of them was a musical play titled *Champaka*, which was staged several times, even outside Visakhapatnam. I recall Shri N.T. Rama Rao, then chief minister of Andhra Pradesh, was present in the audience, when it was staged at Ravindra Bharati in Hyderabad. He had some good things to say about it.

Faculty Position

In 1953, I completed my BA (Hons) course. As I was looking for a career, one of our distant relatives employed in the Intelligence Bureau of Government of India, suggested that I could seek employment in it. I was about ready to take that route. I had little guidance from my father or from my wife's parents. As the destiny would have it, Lakshmana Rao in the

Philosophy Department got a Fulbright scholarship and left for USA. So, there was an unexpected vacancy in the Department, for which I was fully qualified. Prof. Sen immediately took steps to appoint me as a lecturer in the vacancy of Lakshmana Rao. In those days, when there was a good internal candidate, he was automatically recruited on the recommendation of the concerned head without any further fuss, like advertisements and interviews. This system worked well because there was then no bias based on one's caste or other extraneous factors. Merit was the only consideration. There was no nepotism. Public life has since changed much; regrettably morality has taken a back seat, as we are painfully aware.

In the BA (Hons) program, because of small staff in the department, we used to have combined classes in some courses for seniors and juniors. So, when I became a lecturer, some of the students in my class were fellow-students during the previous year. It was therefore not an easy task to assert my identity as a teacher. I began wearing full suit with necktie and all the paraphernalia that gave me a distinct professional look that attracted some attention. Prof. V.S. Krishna was then the vice-chancellor. One day, when he was sitting at the head of the table, I walked into the Faculty Club. He had a good look at me and inquired who I was. That was the first time, he got to know me. Apparently, he was quite impressed by the way I looked.

Prof. Krishna and Dr. N.G. Ranga were together in England as students. When Dr. Ranga visited

Prof. Krishna at the latter's residence during 1953, he inquired about me. So Krishna sent for me; and Ranga told Krishna about our mutual acquaintance in earlier years. Ranga was later elected to parliament from Srikakulam. Whenever he came to visit Srikakulam, he stopped at my house. We often had lunch together at my house.

As a student in the Philosophy Department, I was quite active, and participated regularly in student functions. Shri K.V. Gopalaswamy was the Registrar; and he was a great patron of cultural programs. The present Open Air Theatre is appropriately named after him. Every year in the month of December, Andhra University conducted what were known as the Andhra Week Celebrations. Students from the university and its affiliated colleges actively participated themselves in those competitions, which included elocution contests, staging plays, and a variety of other cultural programs. It so happened, the play in which I had the role of a hero, won the first prize. Since then Gopalaswamy and I got to know each other very well. After becoming a member of the faculty, I used to direct and produce plays for staging during the Andhra Week Celebrations. Prof. B. Satyanarayana Murty of the Law Department was the leading faculty figure in this annual show.

After joining the university as a member of the faculty in 1953, I registered myself for MA (Hons) by research, under the guidance of Prof. Sen. The topic was "Paranormal Cognition: An East–West Study," which was later published under the title *Psi Cognition.*

At my request, J.B. Rhine wrote the Foreword; and I thus got acquainted with Rhine. I was awarded the MA (Hons) degree in 1955.

Those were the days when the young faculty were on the look out to go abroad for higher studies. USA and the UK were favored destinations. I was no exception. So I applied for a Fulbright scholarship to go to USA. I was interviewed in Madras and was selected. The selection was confirmed at the national level and I was advised that I would be sailing from Bombay in June of 1957. I was all set to go; but to my great shock I received a cable from the United States Educational Foundation in India (USEFI) stating that the scholarship was withdrawn because I could not get a placement in the Psychology Department at Duke University.

It was a great disappointment. I had to live with it. When I wrote to Dr. Rhine about it, he replied that he was no longer a regular professor in the Psychology Department and that he had his own set-up within the university but independent of the Psychology Department, known as the Parapsychology Laboratory. The relationship between his establishment and the department was anything but cordial. That was the reason why I could not secure a placement at Duke.

As destiny would have it, Lakshmana Rao was in the USA, Satchidananda Murty was in the UK, and Prof. Sen died. I was the only regular faculty member left in the department. So I became the head. During this period, Prof. Richard McKeon, a distinguished professor of philosophy at the University of Chicago, came to visit Andhra University on behalf of the UNESCO. He naturally came to visit us in the Philosophy Department. I got to know him well as I hosted several events in his honor.

The following year I applied again for a Fulbright Award. This time I was wiser and chose the University of Chicago as the place to study philosophy. I was automatically selected from Madras zone. Surprisingly, however, the recommendation of the regional committee of the Fulbright program was not approved by the national office.

About this time, I also applied for a British Council Fellowship to study with Gilbert Ryle at Oxford University. I was called for an interview by the British Council in Delhi. While I was in New Delhi, I was curious to know why my Fulbright application was rejected at the national level. So, I went to the USIEF office, the one which administered the Fulbright program in India. I met Dr. Olive I. Reddick who was in-charge of the program. I inquired why my application was rejected when it was approved during the previous year. She said that they made a mistake last year; they did not notice that I did not have two years experience after I received my Master's degree as required. I told her pointedly that she was dead wrong. I had the required experience. The BA (Hons) degree is equal to MA. All that one has to do is to pay a small amount to the university and receive the Master's degree automatically. Dr. Reddick immediately recognized that they had made a mistake.

She also knew that I was in Delhi to attend the British Council interview. So, she asked me if I would accept the Fulbright scholarship, if awarded, foregoing the British Council Fellowship. With my interest in parapsychology and eyes focused on meeting Rhine, I told her that I would. She included my name in the selected list of Fulbright scholars and got it approved.

Once again, the hand of destiny. If I had not called on Dr. Reddick, I would possibly have gone to Oxford. It would have dramatically changed my professional course. Man desires; but it is the destiny that dispenses.

2

First Trip to USA

I was awarded the Fulbright scholarship; and sailed from Bombay on a P&O ship coming from Australia in June of 1958. Soon after we left the port and began sailing, we were caught in a storm in the Arabian Sea. The suitcases under our beds in the cabin began rocking back and forth. Many on-board became seasick. I was one of the fortunate ones who was little affected. Once the storm was gone, we were back on our feet moving freely on the deck. It was a single class passenger ship. So we could move freely on the deck from one end to the other. Since we were a contingent of over fifteen Fulbright scholars, we had a gala time. We performed an Indian wedding to entertain fellow travelers, and did several other interesting things.

Our first stop was Aden, a free port at the time. Things were believed to be cheaper there. I had some cash with me, so I bought a baby Hermes typewriter, which I thought would be handy to type my routine class assignments at the university. I used to have it with me until recently.

We then briefly touched Marseilles, South of France, and Gibraltar, and then sailed to Southampton,

England. We traveled from there to London by train; and stayed in a hostel in the India House, maintained by the Indian government, not too far from the Trafalgar Square.

After less than a week in London, we went by train to Liverpool and took the large ship Queen Elizabeth to travel to New York. As we were reaching New York, we could see the majestic statue of liberty. The shores of the city of New York, I found and still value as a true symbol of liberty, political as well as spiritual. From New York, I went to Bennington, Vermont. At Bennington College, the Fulbright scholars from India had an orientation program under the guidance of Brad Smith.

I recall celebrating the Indian Independence Day, hoisting and saluting the Indian flag at Bennington College. I also recall with some amusement a small incident. One of my friends and a fellow Fulbright scholar, Nagaraj, was a strict vegetarian. He promised his parents before leaving India that he would not eat any non-vegetarian food. We were served at a get-together party some refreshments that included vegetarian and non-vegetarian cutlets which looked alike. By mistake, Nagaraj was shown the non-vegetarian dish and told that it was vegetarian. As he was having a bite of the non-vegetarian cutlet, Mrs. Smith saw him and asked him since when did he become a non-vegetarian. Nag was completely stunned. He turned to me with tears in his eyes and said: "Rao garu, I committed the greatest sin of my life. I promised my parents that I would not touch any non-vegetarian food. Now, I had a bite into this. What should I do?" He sobbed and sobbed like a child, and asked me to burn his tongue as a punishment. It took all my counseling skills to convince him that it was not his fault. Sometimes, without knowing, one may swallow some insects. That would not make him a non-vegetarian. What happened to him was something similar. It was no fault of his. I managed to give some relief; but, I knew, he was very disturbed and depressed.

I had about a week free time after the orientation program at Bennington College and before attending the University of Chicago. I decided to go to Durham, NC and visit Rhine at Duke University during that time. I traveled by bus from New York to Durham. As I got down from the bus in Durham, I saw men's rooms clearly marked "white" and "colored." I was going to the toilet room meant for colored people. A white man stopped me and told me that I could use the one meant for white people. I was amused; it was perhaps because of the light color of my skin.

My visit to Duke University gave me a chance to get personally acquainted with J.B. Rhine, his wife Louisa, and his right hand man at the time G.J. Pratt, and also Karlis Osis, Wadih Saleh, W.G. Roll, Charles Tart, and a few others. Rhine told me that I was welcome to visit and spend some time at his laboratory, whenever I found time. It was a kind of open invitation.

As a student at large, I had good time at the University of Chicago. I attended the classes I wanted to; I had no particular schedule. I stayed at the International House on the 59th Street facing the Midway that divided the less attractive and crime-prone south side neighborhood from the university campus. When it snowed and the pavements were slippery, I simply skipped the classes. Sitting in the lounge of the International House, I used to watch and console those who had bad time walking on icy roads returning from their classes. My mentor in the Department of Philosophy was Prof. Richard P. McKeon. I never missed his classes, and acquired some kind of an expertise in his "Historical Semantics." This immensely endeared me to him.

Dr. V.S. Krishna was the Vice-Chancellor of Andhra University at that time. A man of great vision and future perspective, and fully committed to promoting the university's interests, Dr. Krishna was looking for a successor to head Andhra University library, as the librarian at the time was reaching the retirement age. His eyes fell on me. He wanted me to study Library Science at the University of Chicago and get fully qualified to head the Andhra University Library. Since my Fulbright scholarship would expire after one year, he recommended my name for a Rockefeller Foundation Fellowship to enable me to spend one more year at the University of Chicago to take courses in Library Science and get a master's degree in it. He personally knew Dr. Patrick who was the administrator in-charge of the Rockefeller Foundation in India.

Following Dr. Krishna's recommendation, I was called for an interview around Christmas time at the Rockefeller Center in New York. I was staying at the YMCA hostel, located at the 33rd Street. I took a taxi to the Rockefeller Center which was about twenty blocks away. The traffic was moving so slowly that I would have been late for my interview. So, I got out of the cab and walked briskly to the Rockefeller Center, in time for my interview. I was selected. My stipend as a Rockefeller Fellow was significantly more than what I was getting as a Fulbright scholar. Further, I could bring my wife from India; her travel was covered by the fellowship.

So Sarojini joined me in USA. My brother helped her to board the aircraft in Bombay. She left our eldest daughter Rani in India to live with her parents in Kolavennu. I was there in New York to receive her. At that time, Sarojini could not converse in English, but she managed to reach me. We took an apartment close to the University of Chicago on 55th Street. In those days, we had no idea of family planning. My wife soon became pregnant. I now had the additional chores of taking her regularly for medical check-ups and be a translator to her physician. She delivered a beautiful daughter and we named her Vani on 8 April 1960 at the University of Chicago Hospital. Vani is one of the bright jewels in the family. She is loving, brilliant, and gifted in many ways. Currently, she is a practicing neurologist at Duke University Medical Center, USA.

While staying at the International House, not with much academic workload, I had time for extra-curricular activities. I was elected as the President of India Association of Chicago. I had the privilege of presiding over the function to celebrate the Republic Day. John F. Kennedy, who was a senator at the time, was the Chief Guest. He spoke fondly about India, and his admiration for Jawaharlal Nehru. I recall Dr. L. Suryanarayana along with a few others in an Indian medical delegation visiting USA were in the audience. I had a chance to meet him; and this had eventually paved the way for the marriage of my son Sarat with his granddaughter Mridula.

In those days, there was a lot of interest in USA about Hinduism and Indian culture. This was ignited in large part due to Vivekananda and his historic speech at the World Congress of Religions. William James was one of the well-known figures who shared that interest. As the destiny would have it, I was invited to speak on Hinduism on one Sunday at the Rockefeller Chapel by the Chicago Theological Seminary (CTS). This gave me an opportunity to know personally the CTS President. He inquired about me and graciously offered an apartment at the recently built apartment house for married CTS students. So, I was lucky to find a nice, modern apartment with affordable rent. Opposite our apartment lived Guruswamy and his wife Kasturi from Madras Christian College. They took immediate liking to us; and Kasturi became very attached to our little baby, Vani.

Time passed by very quickly. I completed my studies at the University of Chicago. It was time for me to return to India. However, I had a few more months leave left to rejoin Andhra University. I recalled the open invitation of Rhine, and decided to spend a few months with him, before leaving for India. So, I sent my wife and our little daughter Vani back to India; and I went to Durham to spend a few months at Rhine's Parapsychology Laboratory.

I bonded well with Dr. J.B. Rhine and his wife Louisa. They took me several times to their home located amidst woods in nearby Hillsboro. I recall how Rhine chopped wood for the fireplace for use during winter months. He was physically robust. There was a nice pond adjoining their property, a good place for recreation.

On all working days, there used to be at the Parapsychology Laboratory a meeting of staff and research fellows just before lunch time. It was called the Coffee Hour. Rhine used to share his worldwide correspondence; and then an invited speaker or one of the staff or a research fellow would make a presentation. When Rhine was speaking, no one would interrupt him. However, fresh from graduate school with a very inquisitive mind, I began to interrupt and raise all kinds of questions. Rhine, not used to this kind of an interference, could not tolerate this for very long. One day, he stopped me and told me that I should not interrupt. "It is not the way we do things here," he said with some visible annoyance. Young, immature, and somewhat volatile, I got up to leave, saying that the only way to learn well that I knew was to ask questions. If that was not permitted here, this was no place for me to learn. Rhine held my hand, pulled me down to sit, and said that it was not necessary, and that I could ask whatever questions I had in mind. After the meeting, I went to my office; and soon Rhine's trusted and devoted secretary of many years' standing, Fay David, came to my office and told me that Rhine was very upset. She said to Rhine, that he had many friends and should not feel bad about this small incident. She told me, "Dr. Rhine shook his head and said I did not deserve any." She literally begged me to go and see Rhine. In some ways, I felt quite ashamed of myself. I quickly went to see Rhine; and told him how sorry I was for saying what I did. Rhine said, "no, your apology is entirely uncalled for; you are right. Feel free to interrupt me without any hesitation." This attitude of Rhine to correct himself further endeared him to me; and my respect for him grew stronger. I was later informed by some of his colleagues that Rhine was a changed person after that event, and the coffee hours were more interactive.

I should mention, as I went to say goodbye to him on the eve of my departure, Rhine told me that he would like to have me back as a research fellow at his laboratory whenever I chose to return. It was a warm and open invitation.

As I returned to Andhra University, my mentor and the reason behind my studying library science, Dr. V.S. Krishna went to Delhi and took charge as the Chairman of the University Grants Commission (UGC), a very prestigious position. Alas! Hardly a month after he joined the UGC, he had a massive heart attack and died. Now the main motivation behind my studying library science disappeared. My primary interest was in parapsychology and Indian philosophy. Since Dr. Krishna was no longer there, I declined to take charge of the library and openly expressed my desire to rejoin the Department of Philosophy. Prof. C. Mahadevan was then the Principal of the University Colleges. As mentioned, I had a special relationship with him. He rebuked me, and said it was a shame that I was letting him and the university down. The post of University Librarian was kept vacant, waiting for my return. A new building for the library is coming up; it needs supervision. The entire collection of the books in the library needs to be shifted into the new building. Prof. Mahadevan left little choice for me; he made me feel guilty. I reluctantly joined as the University Librarian.

However, I took the job with all seriousness and full sense of responsibility. I helped to complete the construction of the new building, which still stands there, and moved the huge collection into the new building. It was not an easy task, because of the risk of losing books and damaging valuable manuscripts in transit. I had some trusted assistants who were of great help in this. I took the initiative to organize the Department of Library Science and introduce postgraduate courses. In retrospect, I feel quite satisfied with all the work that went into this task. However, I was emotionally drained and physically exhausted; I needed to recoup and re-energize myself to get back to my main academic interest. Then, I recalled Rhine's offer and the open invitation. I conveyed to him my willingness and readiness to return to USA for a stay of few years. Rhine responded positively.

3

Return to USA

I FLEW TO USA ALONG WITH my wife and two kids in June 1962 for a three-year stay at the Parapsychology Laboratory at Duke University as a Research Fellow. With all his manifest kindness in words and warm hospitality at home, Rhine was very stingy when it came to money matters. I was offered a monthly stipend of $7,500 with the proviso to raise it $8,000 during the second year. Even with that meager amount I sent my eldest daughter, Rani, to Durham Academy, a private school, paying $500 as tuition fee. My younger daughter went to Duke Nursery. Since I was a Duke University employee, it did not cost me anything for Vani's nursery school.

Dr. Rhine took his mandatory retirement from Duke when he reached the age of seventy. The stage was set for his leaving Duke in 1965. Rhine was internationally known for his pioneering work in experimental parapsychology. He received significant financial support from several sources ranging from public foundations to private donations. Confident that he could raise enough resources to build and maintain it, Rhine decided to set up his own establishment to promote parapsychology outside the university. He feared that once he leaves Duke, the parapsychology set-up at Duke would be shut down. He bought a nice, old building across the street from the East Campus of Duke University and had set-up his Parapsychology Institute at the corner of North Buchanan Boulevard and Trinity Avenue.

Between 1962 and 1965, a lot of interesting things of tremendous consequence to me and my career had happened. At that time, Dr. D.S. Kothari, an eminent Indian physicist, became the Chairman of the University Grants Commission. He happened to read a review of my book *Psi Cognition* in a little known bulletin *Main Currents*, which reached a few elite intellectuals like him. Dr. Kothari had a strong interest in parapsychology. He was a Jain; and Jainism believed in omniscience, and man's ability to develop paranormal powers. As a scientist, with broad interests that went beyond physics, Dr. Kothari had a lot of interest in scientific research in ESP and such phenomena. He was somewhat familiar with Rhine's work.

Dr. Kothari took time to send me a congratulatory note on the publication of my book *Psi Cognition*. This letter was sent to my Andhra University address. By then, I was in USA on a three-year assignment at Rhine's Parapsychology Laboratory at Duke University. It took a couple of months for the letter to reach me in USA. I immediately wrote back thanking him for his generous, appreciative words. This letter went with my Duke University address. It cheered Dr. Kothari to learn that I was at Duke working with Rhine. He immediately wrote back and asked if I would come back to India and help establish a national Institute of Parapsychology in India. I was delighted at this development; and I asked Rhine to send me to visit India. Rhine was also happy because he was eagerly looking for new places to introduce parapsychology as a subject of academic study and research. So, Rhine agreed to send me to India with funds from his Laboratory. At that time, G.J. Pratt, an associate of Rhine and second in command at his Laboratory was in Japan. Rhine asked Pratt to join me in India and help prepare a report to set-up the Institute of Parapsychology in India.

Along with Pratt, I met Kothari in his office in New Delhi. He asked us to visit several universities in India and to make recommendations for promoting study and research in parapsychology in the country. He made it very clear to me that the institute would be a national level institution with full support and funding from the UGC and the Government of India. He also told me that Dr. Radhakrishnan, then President of India, wanted to hand over the Viceroy's residence in Simla for establishing a national level educational institution; and if we chose Simla as the place to locate the Institute of Parapsychology, the Government of India would be willing to give the Presidential Estate in Simla for locating the new institute. Dr. Kothari arranged for me a lunch meeting with Gulzarilal Nanda, Home Minister of the country then, who also had great interest in *yoga* and its scientific study as in parapsychology. I had lunch with Nandaji at his residence. I recall he ate only dry nuts and some fruits. Then, I was taken to have tea with the Prime Minister, Jawaharlal Nehru.

I was 33 years old and immature in many respects. I only knew Visakhapatnam in India. I did not understand any Hindi. I noticed that Kothari was frequently switching over to Hindi in the middle of conversation. I often had trouble to understand what he was saying. I thought that I would be fish out of water in Simla. After visiting over a dozen universities in India that included Banaras, Lucknow, Mysore, Madras and of course Andhra University, I influenced Pratt to suggest in our report that Andhra University would be the most suitable place. Understandably, this did not please Kothari; but as a true gentleman and committed academician and administrator, he gracefully accepted our recommendation and forwarded the proposal to Andhra University with the UGC pledging for the proposed institute full financial support for five years. This development pleased me immensely; and I was back in USA, hoping that a call would some come from Andhra University for me to return and organize the Institute of Parapsychology. That day did not come. Andhra University simply ignored the UGC proposal to establish the Institute of Parapsychology at Andhra University, and several follow-up reminders.

Puzzled and somewhat disturbed, I returned to India to find out what exactly was happening. I first met Kothari in Delhi. He said that he did everything he could; but received no response from Andhra

University. The universities in India were autonomous bodies and that the UGC could not do anything to coerce them. The UGC could do no more than forward the proposals. He also pointedly mentioned that our proposal did not suggest any alternative institution. The blame was squarely on my shoulders.

From Delhi, I flew to Visakhapatnam and first met the Andhra University Registrar Shri K.V. Gopalaswamy, whom I had known well because of my participation in the cultural activities he organized. He told me very candidly that the vice-chancellor was against the proposal; but he could not say "no" because such a response would receive wide condemnation, which he would be unable to face and contain. Therefore, he was simply sitting over it, hoping that the proposal would slowly die down. The vice-chancellor at that time was Dr. A.L. Narayana, formerly Principal of a college in Vizianagaram. He was caste conscious, petty minded, highly prejudicial person with no scruples. He had no long-term interest of the university while taking his decisions. Narayana was telling people that the proposed institute with its autonomy would be a university within the university and that such a proposal was simply unacceptable to him.

To say the least, A.L. Narayana was a controversial figure. His appointment was political; and it was opposed by many within and outside the university. He was facing a lot of opposition. He, however, was stubbornly sticking to his job with a few members of the Syndicate (Executive Council) of the university continuing their support to him. One of his supporters was Kancherla Sreerama Murty, an elected member of AP State Legislative Assembly. Sreerama Murty was my former student; and he received several favors from me. So, on a friend's advice, I met Sreerama Murty and told him about what was happening. Immediately, he called on the vice-chancellor and told him that the university should accept the UGC proposal. The vice-chancellor responded by saying that there was no accommodation available at Andhra University to house the proposed institute. Therefore, he could not accept the proposal. Smartly, Sreerama Murty informed him that he had a house near the university and that he would give it to locate the institute. So, Dr. Narayana had no choice but to accept, because Sreerama Murty's support was very crucial for his survival at the university. So, finally Andhra University communicated to the UGC its acceptance of the proposal to locate the Institute of Parapsychology at Andhra University.

The above development paved the way for my return to India. I shared all this information with J.B. Rhine and informed him of my wish to return to India and sought his help to organize the institute. Rhine was not quite pleased with my decision. He wanted me to stay on in USA. With his impending retirement from Duke and his plans to build the Institute of Parapsychology outside of Duke University under the auspices of the newly established Foundation for Research on the Nature of Man (FRNM), he felt that he needed me. I persisted on my desire and decision to go back to India. Rhine was visibly upset. We had rather heated arguments.

As I prepared to leave for India, I asked Rhine if I could have one of the calculating machines. He had many of them in his Lab, and several of them not being used at all. I thought Rhine would readily agree; but he said "no," pointing out that he had nothing when he started, and that I should do the same and acquire my own.

By the time of my leaving, I completed writing my book *Experimental Parapsychology: A Review and Interpretation* to be published by Charles C. Thomas, who published earlier Rhine and Pratt's textbook. I asked Rhine to write the Foreword to this book. In the background of my leaving for India despite his reservations, he wrote a somewhat indifferent Foreword, quite in contrast with the praise he showered on me when he first read the manuscript. I was understandably upset. I discarded his Foreword and got the book published without it.

When I left Rhine's establishment, I had very little savings. However, I managed to buy an electric calculating machine made in Sweden and took it with me to India and presented it to the newly-created Department of Psychology and Parapsychology at Andhra University.

Now, we may recall, the UGC funding was meant for setting up the Institute of Parapsychology. Why did I prefer calling it the Department of Psychology and Parapsychology? There were several reasons behind it. First, I thought, the divide between psychology and parapsychology was artificial. It needed to be bridged. Rhine's negative tryst with the Psychology Department at Duke University had something to do with its isolation from Duke. Rhine entertained the presumption that people in the Psychology Department at Duke were personally opposed to him. I knew that he was wrong. I was acquainted with several people in the Psychology Department of Duke personally, including Dr. Gutman who was perceived as a bitter critic of Rhine and parapsychology. I recall that S.H. Mauskopf, who along with M.R. McVaugh (1980) wrote the book titled *Elusive Science* chronicling the history of parapsychology at Duke University, was scheduled to give a public lecture in the Department of Psychology, Parapsychology as the backdrop. Rhine was very reluctant to attend the meeting. However, I persuaded and drove him and his wife with me to the lecture. It was a truly memorable experience. As we entered the lecture hall, there was a thunderous standing applause; and I never saw such happiness in Rhine's face. There was indeed a relish of satisfaction radiating, and realization that his long effort was not lost in the history of psychology at Duke.

Second, I wanted parapsychology not merely as a subject for research but as a subject to be taught as a branch of psychology like, for example, abnormal psychology. This could be best accomplished by combining the two names together. This arrangement on the one hand would give parapsychology its own identity, and show on the other hand its close affinity with psychology.

Third, I had a special interest in *yoga*. I thought all along that *yoga* had something to offer to psychology in general and parapsychology in particular. Further, *yoga* needed a scientific orientation for its study, and parapsychology could provide it. Thus, I saw a reciprocal relationship between Parapsychology and Yoga.

The Department of Psychology and Parapsychology was inaugurated at Andhra University on a beautiful day in December of 1967. It has been in existence now for over fifty years. Before, the department was formally inaugurated, by accident, as mentioned earlier, I served as the Chief Librarian of Andhra University. With over eighty people working in the library, I had a large workforce. My connections with the top officials in the university and the members of the Syndicate (Executive Council) helped me to yield significant influence in university matters. I came to know very intimately Shri Ramakrishna Prasad, one of the important and effective members of the university syndicate. We remained lifelong friends.

I had two PhD students who returned with me from Duke, and remained my loyal students and warm friends on whom I could count for any support. They were given due accommodation in the library for their offices and study. Prof. Srinivasa Iyengar, who was a true academician and a great scholar and expert in English literature and Indian English, used to live opposite my house on the Andhra University campus.

His house was at somewhat a lower level across the street. He used to joke, "Prof. Rao, we look up to you." I gently would say, "Sir, I bow down before you." Prof. Iyengar unexpectedly succeeded A.L. Narayana as the vice-chancellor. He appointed me as Honorary Professor of Psychology; and I was asked to continue as the University Librarian as well. This arrangement lasted until Shri L. Bullayya took over as the vice-chancellor. Bullayya asked me to choose one of the two, library or the department. I happily chose to head the Department of Psychology and Parapsychology. We moved our offices into the present convocation hall, occupying the rooms in the front and the rear of the building. My office used to be in the large front room on the east side of the building.

With the financial help from the UGC, we soon had our own building for offices, classrooms, and labs. I have had a special aptitude for nice and clean surroundings. When I was heading the library, for the first time in the university, we had grown a nice garden surrounding the building. I ensured that the library building was kept clean, including the book racks. The attender would no longer sit on a stool and wait for a student to ask for help to find a book. Instead, he was made to constantly dust and ensure that the books were in the precise order so that they could be easily located. Students were encouraged to browse; we had a free access system.

Once the Department of Psychology and Parapsychology had its own building, I ensured that it was the cleanest on campus and an attractive structure in the university. I provided all the necessary facilities; and entrusted the job of keeping the building clean to a class IV employee I picked up, Pydamma. She zealously safe-guarded my wish to be clean and green. She scrupulously followed my instructions. She would not allow any student or even a faculty member with dirty shoes walking into the building on a rainy day without first removing the shoes. Since she had my full support, all those entering the building followed her instructions without making any fuss.

On the terrace of the building we grew flowering plants, mostly roses I brought from Bangalore and other parts of the country I visited. Many walked to the terrace to see the roses; but none touched them. On some evenings, I myself sat on the terrace, enjoying the colour and fragrance of the roses. In some ways, I was an autocrat; but the best part was that it worked.

I am used to luxuries in my living. I had expensive steel furniture in my office obtained from Bombay. Bullayya, Vice-Chancellor, who saw it when he came to visit me one day in my office, ordered similar furniture for his use in his office. The other day, when I visited the Yoga Village, I found the same table I had as the Head of the Department now being used by the present Director of the Department of Yoga and Consciousness. Our seminar room was tastefully decorated. We had portraits of renowned psychologists drawn by B. Prasad one of our faculty members who was very gifted in making them. With comfortable chairs and custom-made long tables, our seminar hall was a model, one envied by other departments in the university.

The department attracted students in good numbers; and most of them happened to be beautiful young ladies from well-to-do, educated families. So the department was a special attraction to male students from other departments in the university with the result we had no difficulty in recruiting subjects for participating in our experiments.

I started a laboratory to study nocturnal dreaming. The subject had to sleep all night in the laboratory. Our staff collected dream reports, waking up the subject soon after the REM period, which indicated that he was dreaming. We had no dearth of subjects! Our department and the dream laboratory became well known in the student community.

The dream laboratory at Andhra University was one of the earliest in the country. We had a 14-channel electroencephalograph (EEG) machine with full polygraph facilities. We imported it from Japan. This was made possible by a substantial grant I received from Parapsychology Foundation (PF). The Foundation was created and developed by Mrs. Eileen Garrett, a grand old lady, who earlier practiced mediumship in UK. I first met Mrs. Garrett along with Karlis Osis who was then the director of research at PF, located in New York city, before I joined Rhine. Ours was love at first sight.

PF supported Rhine financially for a while. However, Rhine and Garrett had their differences.

During my period at Rhine's laboratory I had little contact with PF. However, after returning to India, I renewed my contacts with PF and got to know well Mrs. Garrett, Karlis Osis, and Alan Angoff, the Administrative Officer at PF. We all got along very well. The PF used to have annually an international conference at Le Piol, in a hotel by that name owned by Mrs. Garrett in South of France, close to Nice. I was frequently invited to these conferences. My association with PF remained even after Mrs. Garrett passed away. I kept in touch with her daughter Mrs. Coly and her granddaughter Lissette Coly. PF at one time was one of the main supporters of parapsychological research around the world. It had one of the finest parapsychology-related book collection. Unfortunately, after Mrs. Garrett, PF gradually disintegrated. It did not attract the funding it needed; and had gradually become financially weak, now in need of support for its own survival.

I had several postgraduate students working in the dream laboratory. A few of them wrote their PhD dissertations on nocturnal dreaming. How I wish this work had continued! With my leaving Andhra University, the dream laboratory was closed, as there was no one to lead and find the necessary financial support to maintain it.

4

Unexpected Twists and Turns
Again, the Hand of Destiny

TO GET BACK TO OUR STORY, things were going well for me at Andhra University. The Department of Psychology and Parapsychology enjoyed a prestigious place in the university. My role in the university had become more diversified. I was elected as the Dean of Faculty of Arts, which included social sciences. I was also elected as a member of the Syndicate (Executive Council) of the university from the Academic Council in which all university professors and a large number of principals of colleges affiliated to Andhra University were members. The Academic Council's jurisdiction covered the entire area of the present state of Andhra Pradesh, post-bifurcation. So, I represented a fairly large constituency.

While the department was well set to take off, and I was ready to play significant leadership role in the management of Andhra University, a distress call (SOS) came from J.B. Rhine, my mentor in parapsychology. As mentioned, Rhine moved his Parapsychology Laboratory out of Duke University and started his Institute of Parapsychology sponsored by the Foundation for Research on the Nature of Man

(FRNM). He selected J. Levy, a bright young medical graduate to head the institute. Levy began publishing extensively research reports on his work with animals. The basement of FRNM had an animal lab. Levy's assistants became suspicious of the way Levy handled the data. They duly reported their apprehensions about the validity of Levy's data. Rhine was one of those who never compromised over the integrity of the data coming from his lab. Any weakness on his part in this regard could have ruined his reputation and career, considering the widespread and well-trenched criticism of his work. Rhine immediately fired Levy. This was national news covered among others by the *Time* magazine.

Following this deplorable incident, Rhine was looking for a substitute in place of Levy. It just so happened that I was at this time in USA to attend a small parapsychology gathering sponsored by the Parapsychology Foundation in Santa Barbara, CA. The annual convention of the Parapsychological Association (PA) was also held at that time in Santa Barbara, I took the opportunity to attend the PA Convention. Charles Honorton, an young, gifted and energetic person fully committed to parapsychology from almost his childhood was the President of PA. He joined Rhine's FRNM and was active as a research scientist. Then, he had differences with Rhine. He engineered a revolt, pulling out of FRNM several young research associates along with him, causing a major setback to Rhine's establishment in Durham.

In his opening statement as President of the Convention, Honorton referred to the events at the FRNM, the Levy affair, and his decision not to accept any papers submitted by FRNM staff for presentation at the PA Convention. I was really upset at this statement. As it happened, I did a little piece of work while at the FRNM and submitted a paper based on my work. It was accepted for presentation at that convention. I raised my hand from the audience. Honorton recognized me. I stood up and strongly protested at what he had said. Without mincing any words, I pointed out that he had no right to exercise such censorship. My statement was greeted with a loud applause. Dr. Gertrude Schmeidler, a pioneering parapsychologist well known for the sheep–goat effect she investigated, also spoke in support of what I had said.

This news must have reached Rhine. Rhine called and asked me to visit FRNM before I left for India. So, I stopped briefly at FRNM. Rhine offered me the position of Director of the Institute of Parapsychology and tried to persuade me to return to Durham in the overall interest of parapsychology worldwide. He said that I was the right one to lead and unite the different factions in the field. I told Rhine that I was not ready to return to USA. Our department at Andhra University is all set to take off, and it would be unwise to leave it at that time. Rhine was not a man who would easily give up. He pointed out that the stakes were very high; and that it was a perilous period for the field itself. I told Rhine I would think it over and let him know my decision after returning to India.

On return, I thought about it for several days. It seemed okay for me to leave Andhra University for a few years, entrusting the responsibility of the Department of Psychology and Parapsychology to Prof. S. Parthasarathy, a professor of psychology, just retired from S.V. University, who visited us earlier at Duke, and had shown some interest in parapsychology. To facilitate this move, I offered a position to his daughter in the Department of Psychology and Parapsychology at Andhra University.

I informed Rhine that I would be happy to join his Institute of Parapsychology, taking work leave from Andhra University for a period of three years. Andhra University had always been kind and generous to me. I was granted leave for three years. I went to USA on exchange visitor's visa; and there was the headache of renewing it frequently. So Rhine suggested that I apply for permanent residence and he sponsored my application. It hardly took two months to get the so-called green card.

While I was at the Institute of Parapsychology, first J.B. Rhine and then Louisa Rhine died; and the burden of leading FRNM fell squarely on my shoulders. I could not return to Andhra University as planned; but the university extended my leave. It had become increasingly clear that I could not leave FRNM and return to India, and that it would be unfair to continue to extend my leave. So I decided to seek formal voluntary retirement from Andhra University; and returned to India to personally tender my resignation. On 4 October 1982 at the age of 50, I took voluntary retirement from Andhra University and said farewell to my alma mater on my 50th birthday. It was a heartbreaking decision but I had to take it.

I recall very vividly the farewell function arranged at the Ersquine Square now named after K.V. Gopalaswamy, a long-time Registrar of Andhra University. The speakers sitting on the dias included Prof. Satchidananda Murty, my teacher and a long time friend and well wisher, Prof. S.P. Adinarayana, a distinguished psychologist and the then Vice-Chancellor of Annamalai University, and Shri M. Venkaiah Naidu, then MLA and now the Vice-President of India. Justice Avula Sambasiva Rao, formerly Chief Justice of Andhra Pradesh and at that time Vice-Chancellor of Andhra University presided over the function. It was emotionally difficult to say goodbye to Andhra University, which was in a significant sense my academic other; but I had to. Taking retirement from Andhra University, I returned to Durham to resume my responsibilities as the Director of the Institute of Parapsychology. I thought that we would settle down in USA for good.

We bought a house in the prestigious Hope Valley in the area of Durham. William Roll and his wife Muriel lived in the same street. They had two children. Sarojini and I became very fond of them, especially their daughter Lisa. Not very far from us and in the same neighborhood lived Reddy Parvata and his family. Reddy and I used to play tennis. We became close friends; so close that we jointly owned some real estate in Durham. Reddy and Vimala still live in the same house.

We had the privilege of hosting several dignitaries at our home. The first lady of Mexico came to visit us because of her interest in parapsychology. This also brought Jim Hunt, then Governor of North Carolina to our house. This attracted a lot of attention in the neighborhood; and in some ways our stock went up.

We had very good neighbors. On the west side of our home lived a lady psychiatrist. On the east side, it was mostly a wooded area. So was our backside on the north. We were pretty secluded but in a secure neighborhood. I added a porch at the back of the house which opened up to our backyard. We had a three car garage, which we did not really need. So we created an additional bedroom out of it. Next to it on the western side we had the family room.

Durham is not very far from High Point, which was considered at the time the furniture capital of the world. Now, of course, the Chinese took over. We bought a lot of good furniture and tastefully decorated the house. Much of that furniture we brought along with us when we made our final move to India.

5

Back to Andhra University

MAN PROPOSES; BUT it is destiny that disposes. Again, destiny took over. Shri N.T. Rama Rao, a popular film star and known as NTR, disillusioned by the existing political parties and disgusted with the corrupt leadership, started his own political party called Telugu Desam. He won the Assembly elections with a landslide verdict. He was determined to provide the best possible governance. Towards this end, he began to look around for talented people to head various institutions. NTR asked Justice Sambasiva Rao to head the legal outfit of the government he created to oversee the legal institutions in the state and ensure that the government functioned without a semblance of corruption. Consequently, there arose the vacancy of the position of Vice-Chancellor at Andhra University. NTR asked Justice Sambasiva Rao to suggest a suitable name to succeed him as the Vice-Chancellor of Andhra University. Apparently, Justice Rao had recommended my name.

I recall that our family members and some of our relatives living in USA had gathered at our house in Durham, NC to celebrate the Thanksgiving Day. Then, I received a call from Hyderabad. A government official told me that NTR wanted to appoint me as the Vice-Chancellor of Andhra University and that he would like me to return to India immediately. I told him, "Sorry! I am not interested in returning to India; I am well settled in the US." Next day, I had another call from Hyderabad. This time the chief minister himself was on the phone. He offered me the position at Andhra University and asked me to return to India. I politely declined saying that I just took retirement from Andhra University. I also added that Dr. Gopalakrishna Reddy, then Registrar, was a very capable person and that the government could consider him for that position. NTR said angrily that Gopalakrishna Reddy met him with a dozen or so professors canvassing for the job. The Vice-Chancellor position is not something to canvass for but one that needs to be conferred on eminent persons, he added. So he did not think that Gopalakrishna Reddy was the right person for the job. He further said, "I am not taking a no from you; I want you to come and head Andhra University"; and he hung up.

I did not know how to handle the situation. So I consulted Dr. Russell Moores, the Chairman of the FRNM Board of Directors for guidance. Moores said thoughtfully "Andhra University gave you earlier leave for several years to enable you to work at the FRNM. It is now the FRNM's turn to grant you leave to work at Andhra." He offered to recommend to the FRNM Board that I might be given a three-year leave of absence to go back to India and head Andhra University. However, he did not want a new director to take over my job at the FRNM. I would continue to be the director and return to FRNM for a month every year and that I would distribute the work to be done during my absence among three of the senior FRNM staff, John Palmer, Richard Broughton, and H. Kanthamani. With the above arrangement in place, I returned to Andhra University in June of 1984 to function as its Vice-Chancellor. Indeed, it was a rare privilege that I was heading simultaneously two institutions, located continents apart.

My return to Visakhapatnam did not go well with Gopalakrishna Reddy, who was serving as the Andhra University Registrar at that time, and his coterie, even though I had a long-standing positive relationship bordering on friendship with him. At the time, Gopalakrishna Reddy had a *guru* who guided him in every step, as I came to understand. In my view, the *guru* was a scamp. Gopalakrishna Reddy and his *guru* came to see me in Durham, NC, when they were in USA earlier. Other friends shared with me their opinion that the so-called *guru* was a crook and that Reddy was being misguided and taken for a ride by him. I tried to warn Reddy about his unscrupulous *guru*. Reddy was so blinded by his faith in him that he told me that those who criticized his *guru* had lost their eyesight. I was stunned, and felt totally helpless and sorry for his blind faith that eventually distorted his career and in some ways destroyed his life.

On arrival in Visakhapatnam, I came to know that the *guru* prompted Gopalakrishna Reddy to organize a group of students to protest against my appointment.

They planned a black flag demonstration when I arrived to take charge as the Vice-Chancellor. Since I had a good job in USA and was coming reluctantly to India, once I felt the heat, they felt, I would go back to USA.

There was a media blitz that NTR was importing someone from USA to head Andhra University, ignoring the qualified local people. Some student leaders were gifted motor cycles and asked to organize protest demonstrations when I arrived. As I landed in Visakhapatnam, I was received at the airport by my father and my teacher and later colleague Prof. Satchidananda Murty. There were of course dozens of students outside the gate shouting slogans "Go back! Go back!" The Registrar of the University, who should have been at the airport to receive the new Vice-Chancellor, was conspicuous by his absence.

This was not something that I was not expecting. The previous evening, I was fully briefed by the intelligence personnel in Hyderabad. Early in the morning, before I left for Visakhapatnam I met the Chief Minister, N.T. Rama Rao. It was our first meeting. He warmly embraced me and said with his characteristic dialogue delivery: "Please go and rule Andhra University. The Government of Andhra Pradesh is fully behind you." With that kind of assurance from the Chief Minister himself, I became more confident than ever and was ready to face any challenges. As we were driving from the airport, the Registrar stopped our car and met me half way on the road and drove with us to the university. He said that he was locked up in his office by students and that he somehow managed to escape. If this were true, it was entirely stage managed.

We drove directly to the Assembly Hall of Andhra University where I was to address the gathering of faculty and students. Some professors first spoke at the meeting warmly welcoming me. As I stood up to speak, some students at the back began shouting "Go back! Go back!" Responding, I said solemnly, "Yes, I will go back." There was utter silence and a surprise look at me by the faculty sitting in the front rows. I continued "Yes, I will go back; but only after cleaning up all these ugly cobwebs, and after putting the university back on its rails following the great tradition bequeathed by C.R. Reddy, Radhakrishnan, and V.S. Krishna." There was a thunderous applause. I briefly shared with the audience my agenda for action during the next three years.

I was temporarily staying with my sister and brother-in-law at their house in Waltair. An elderly gentleman, Chairman of the West Godavari District Board, came to see me unannounced. He was curious to know whether I knew any Telugu at all. After meeting me, he became one of my ardent supporters. He arranged for a fabulous reception at C.R. Reddy College in Eluru of which he was the chairman, and facilitated me lavishly.

My stay at Andhra University as its Vice-Chancellor had gone by rather peacefully after not so peaceful a beginning. The student leaders who protested reconciled. As the Vice-Chancellor, I bore no ill-will to anyone. I could have humiliated the Registrar. On the contrary, I treated him with more respect than what was due to a Registrar. My positive approach paid rich dividends. Those were days when university campuses were hot beds of protests, strikes, and political interference. Andhra University campus was relatively peaceful. I was free to bring about some administrative changes, curricular reforms, and set-up necessary machinery for promoting quality research in the different departments on campus, and help encourage effective teaching in colleges affiliated to the university.

We created new positions of deans, going beyond academic subjects. We had deans for student affairs, finances, examinations, and so on. Further, we arranged for senior faculty to give extension lectures in colleges affiliated to the university that were spread around the length and breadth of the entire state. This evoked a lot of good response. We also sought to provide greater autonomy to colleges that seemed to show good governance and enduring corporate management. Thus, the Andhra University colleges and the undergraduate colleges affiliated to it were seen as not isolated institutions but organically related entities enriching each other.

My second daughter Vani told me before I left for Visakhapatnam to take charge of Andhra University, "Daddy, when you go there, people will praise you, and speak a lot of good things about you. What is important is what they think of you after you leave."

When I arrived, I was not so warmly received; but when I left, the railway platform was filled with Andhra University people bidding me one of the most affectionate farewells I ever received. So, it was a very satisfying time.

I left Andhra University a few months before I completed my term of three years. While I was the Vice-Chancellor, N.T. Rama Rao, the Chief Minister of Andhra Pradesh, appointed me as the Chairman of the Committee to suggest ways of reorganizing universities in the state. Based on our report, the Government of Andhra Pradesh had created what is now called the A.P. State Council of Higher Education. The central point of our recommendations was that the universities in the state should be headed by academicians and not by bureaucrats or politicians, as it was the practice in vogue at that time. NTR appointed me as its first chairman. So, I had to move to Hyderabad.

Then, my commitment to NTR was that I would stay in India for a period of three years and then return to USA to rejoin the Institute of Parapsychology. The three-year period was nearly over. However, NTR persuaded me to stay a little longer and put the State Council on its rails. So, I stayed on for another six months in Hyderabad before going back to USA.

N.T. Rama Rao arranged a farewell party for me on the eve of my departure to USA at the Jubilee Hall in Hyderabad. All the Vice-Chancellors in the state and several luminaries and high-ranking officials were in attendance. With almost tears in his eyes, NTR told the gathering that his younger brother was leaving him. He wanted my continued advice to help the state, even if I were not physically present in Hyderabad.

In my response at the end, I profusely thanked NTR and others in the government who supported and helped me immensely to do my job. I told them that I had no choice but return to USA because the institute I was heading was without a required substitute. However, I would come back later, if I was asked to return; and then would stay back in India as long as NTR would want me.

6

Two Decades Heading the Institute of Parapsychology

I RETURNED TO USA and rejoined the Institute of Parapsychology six months later than what was originally planned. My stay in Durham, NC, lasted this time for nearly two decades without any major interruption. Now, I had not only the responsibility of conducting and guiding research but also of raising resources for the FRNM. I received of course much help and guidance from the Directors of the Board. They included Chester Carlson, inventor of Xerography, and Clement Stone, then President of the Combined Insurance Corporation of America. Dr. Russell Moores of Georgia Medical College was the Chairman of the Board of Directors. Other financial supporters included Mrs. Higbee, Ms Maurin, and several others who willed their estates to the FRNM.

J.B. Rhine and his wife Louisa gifted to FRNM part of their estate, about 200 acres of land. However, their will and testament had a proviso that the land should not be developed, but remain green as forest land. It was a beautiful piece of land, Eno River flowing through it. While we all valued and appreciated this gift, it was of little financial benefit to the FRNM.

I thought about how we could generate some financial support from it. It occurred to me that we could explore with the state of North of Carolina whether we might exchange it for some other land belonging to the state in that area. It came to my notice that there was an attractive piece of land with a little cottage on top of a hill in nearby Hillsboro township, which belonged to the state government. My negotiations with the state of North Carolina officials were fruitful; and we exchanged the land gifted by the Rhines with the Hillsboro property, which could be developed. This was a big relief. The land gifted by the Rhines would remain green as a part of the state forest.

Mrs. Higbee, who lived in her mansion next door to FRNM building in Durham, gave significant financial support from her own resources. She also willed her house to FRNM as a gift after her death. It would have been ideal for me to live in it, as the Director of the Institute. However, I thought that it may be construed as conflict of interest. So, after her death, we put up the house in the open market for sale; and sold it at a price I could have easily afforded. I did not purchase it because I feared that it might be misconstrued.

There was another lady by name Elizabeth, a benefactor of FRNM, whom Sarojini and I came to know rather intimately. She stayed a few times at our home when she visited Durham. She grew so fond of us that she wanted to leave her estate to us after her death. We, however, suggested and convinced her that her assets should go to the FRNM and not to any individuals. She reluctantly agreed.

We moved from the apartment we were staying into a house located at Huron Circle in Durham. Several friends including the Rhines and Mrs. Higbee were there at the house-warming function. Mrs. Higbee brought with her an expensive porcelain dinner set as a gift to us. I felt not only embarrassed but also some conflict of interest in accepting that gift. So I politely refused to accept the gift and told her that whatever she wants to give should go to the FRNM and not to me. J.B. Rhine gleefully looked at me, taking some pride at the commitment I had shown for the FRNM. His confidence in me as his successor was considerably strengthened.

During my earlier stint at the FRNM, I was very productive as a researcher. I published several papers reporting the results obtained in a number of experiments we conducted. All these studies followed the Rhinean model and focused on what I first called the preferential effect and later more broadly designated as the differential effect. Now with the responsibility of running the FRNM on my shoulders, I could hardly conduct any experimental studies on my own; I had to depend on others. Further, my mind became less restricted to the Rhinean paradigm of psi. I began to think more broadly, relating psi to basic human nature and especially consciousness studies. The evolution of my thinking and the broadening the scope of psi in my mind may be seen by the different kinds of slant and emphasis that could be found in the three successive addresses I gave to the Parapsychological Association (PA) as its elected president, first in 1965 and last in 1990, covering a span of twenty-five years.

In the first address given on 9 September 1965, entitled "The Bidirectionality of Psi," I dealt almost exclusive with my studies of the differential effect and its theoretical implications within the Rhinean paradigm. Interestingly, however, I concluded the address with a few paragraphs on psi in the Indian tradition, especially *yoga*, just reminding myself of my Indian heritage; and there was no more. In my second Presidential Address to the PA with the title "Psi and Its Place in Nature" dated 9 August 1978, I attempted to draw the broader contours of psi. The third address published in 1991 was devoted to exploring the relationship between consciousness studies and psi. My more recent work in this area was devoted to understanding psi–*yoga*–consciousness nexus (see *Cognitive Anomalies, Consciousness and Yoga*, 2011).

With the deaths of J.B. Rhine in 1980 and L.E. Rhine in 1983, in addition to raising funds for the FRNM and running the Institute of Parapsychology and finding resources for it, as mentioned, I had the added responsibility of being the senior editor of the *Journal of Parapsychology*. So I kept myself very busy, fully occupied by many-sided responsibilities. While Sarojini and I along with our son lived in Durham, NC, my two daughters were left behind in Visakhapatnam under the wings of my father, who took care of them better than I could have. With strong family ties in

India and equally strong professional commitments in USA, life was not easy for me.

Rani and Vani attended St. Joseph's College for Women in Visakhapatnam. Rani specialized in home science. Home-making has been her main occupation since. Vani since her childhood wanted to be a physician. She worked very hard for it. She was a meritorious student receiving merit scholarships from the very first year in college. She did her MBBS at Andhra Medical College, Visakhapatnam. All this was happening while I was living in USA. Again, it was the destiny which took care of them.

In our family tradition at that time, marriages were generally arranged by the parents. The children were of course consulted and their preferences were taken into account. Rani was by then of marriageable age. So, I began thinking about it. I returned to India on a short visit and looked around for a suitable groom. Dr. L. Bullayya was at that time Vice-Chancellor of Andhra University. His wife Samyukta was well known to our family. She suggested that we consider Dr. Sarath Gangavarapu, the second son of Smt. Vanajakshi who was then working as a manager of Andhra Bank. We arranged to see him at the house of my cousin Y.V. Subba Rao in Secunderabad, and settled the marriage. Sarath and Rani happily live now in Chattanooga, Tennessee in USA. Sarath is a practicing psychiatrist. They have two lovely daughters. Kavya is married to Pranay; and they live in Atlanta. Shilpa works in New York with a multinational bank. Kavya gave birth to a son in early July 2018. So, we now have an adorable great-grandson, my fourth generation.

Next was the turn of Vani. She just completed her MBBS at Andhra Medical College. She was living in Visakhapatnam in our house in the university under the care of my father, as mentioned.

Dr. Chilukuri Santaram did his postgraduate studies in physics at Andhra University, but settled in USA. He was then looking around for a suitable bride to his eldest son Murali Mohan, who was by then a trained physician. Santaram came to know about us and Vani. There were several others who showed interest in an alliance with us. We have arranged for one of the boys to see Vani on a particular evening to explore possible marriage alliance. Santaram came along with Murali to our house a little earlier than the others on the same day without any prior notice. They met me and Vani. They seemed to like Vani, and Vani was also positively inclined. However, Santaram wanted a little more time to think it over. I told him bluntly that another person is coming to see Vani later in the evening and that I cannot promise to wait. Murali intervened and said that they need not wait and that he was ready to propose. So, the marriage was settled; I telephoned to the other party about it and cancelled the scheduled appointment in the evening. Again, it was the hand of destiny. Who knows what would have happened if Santaram did not drop in at our house unscheduled!

Vani had to wait for some more time in

Visakhapatnam to complete her internship, after which she joined her husband in Maddisonville, Kentucky. Maddisonville area was a small rural community in USA with old values. The physicians in hospital were looked up with much respect. I recall some people used to present home-grown vegetables to Vani. Vani, who first lived in a small house, soon got a huge impressive mansion built for her residence on the side of a lake. She always displayed a taste for good living. It was the place where Dr. Panduranga Rao and his wife Ganga came to see my son Sarat, whom we call Chandu, and proposed alliance with their daughter Mridula, known as Madhu. We all happily agreed. My son and Madhu have two adorable kids, Mira and Tarun. They now live in Carmel, a suburb of Indianapolis. My son is currently the CEO of a company that owns several hundred fast-food outlets.

Now, Vani and Murali have two gifted children, Vivek and Sunila. Both of them graduated from Kennedy School at Harvard. Vivek had worked for a while in the White House when Obama was the President. If Hillary Clinton won, Vivek would have been chosen for an important assignment. Ambassador to India won't have been an appropriate position. Vivek specialized in Mideastern Studies. Sunila, who visited several West African countries, has an expertise in the study of those areas.

To get back to our story, after Vani's wedding, Sarojini and I returned along with our son to Durham and I rejoined FRNM and the Institute of Parapsychology. We bought a home in Hope Valley, a prestigious neighborhood in Durham, and lived there for the rest of our stay in Durham.

During the two decades of my stay in Durham, heading the Institute of Psychology, my first task was to reactivate research. This needed recruiting new staff. When Honorton revolted against Rhine and left the FRNM, he took along with him the rest of the research staff. Hardly anyone was left to carry out research. Further, FRNM used to conduct a summer program annually to provide instruction in parapsychology. The summer school was very popular attracting students not only from different parts of USA but also a few from abroad. After the coupe by Honorton et al. the summer school was in shambles.

I looked around for new recruits. Dr. H. Kanthamani, my former student and colleague, married Hanumantha Rao. Hanu was a student in the Department of Psychology and Parapsychology at Andhra University. Kantha was then living in Durham with her husband. Hanu did his doctoral work in psychology later at North Carolina State University in Raleigh and joined the NC Department of Correction. I invited Kantha to join FRNM's Institute of Parapsychology. Then, there was Richard Broughton who returned from UK and was looking for employment. He had shown some interest in parapsychology; but little work behind him. He was a student of John Beloff at Edinburgh, and did not at the time have any association with Honorton and others who left the FRNM. So, I offered a research position to Broughton. Soon, John Palmer also joined. There were already Jim Kennedy, Mellissa Morrison, and Jim Davis. Davis used to look after the huge IBM computer set-up we had. John Freeman was living in Durham area; and I offered him a position at the Institute. So, I had assembled a full contingent of staff at different levels. Research was back in full swing.

Along with research, we were active at the FRNM on the teaching front as well. We revived the summer school program. Also, we had several interns who stayed on to continue their work in parapsychology. We had a hotline; people could call us and report any extraordinary experiences they had. An assistant was in place to record if anyone reported any special, noteworthy experience, or made a prediction of some consequence. It so happened that a person had reported that she was having a dream repeatedly during the past few nights about the crash of a passenger airplane in Chicago. Sadly, this did actually happen a few days after we received this call. It was a truly startling experience, a true real life episode of precognition.

Even though I could not carry out any experimental studies on my own, I was much involved with research activities at the institute. I co-authored over twenty-five experimental studies published in professional journals during that period. In addition, I published several papers discussing the implications of parapsychological research to other areas. One of the important review papers I brought out with

John Palmer as co-author was entitled "The Anomaly Called Psi." It appeared in the prestigious mainstream journal *The Behavioral and Brain Sciences* (Rao and Palmer 1987), as a target article. The comments of dozens of scientists on this paper and our responses to them were also published in it. Over all, the article had a positive impact; a satisfying experience for me that our work had received well-deserved attention from scientists in general around the world.

Our research was no longer confined to proving the existence of psi in various modalities as in ESP and PK. It was process-oriented. We tried to find out how ESP manifests and investigate its relation to other cognitive abilities, like memory, subliminal perception, and volitional activities. I was also interested in finding out how the normal and the paranormal interact in our daily lives. Further, the matter of cultivating psi by such means as hypnosis and meditation was of considerable interest. Another innovation in testing for ESP was the use of language ESP cards. Crossing the language barrier by ESP was presented as a challenging task; and the subjects responded with significant interest that sustained their motivation to participate in our experiments. My colleagues H. Kanthamani and Shanti Prasad were actively involved in these experimental studies of what we termed language ESP.

To return to our story, Vani and Murali moved from Madisonville to Chapel Hill so as to live closer to us. They had by then two kids; and Sarojini was taking care of them after school hours. Vani has expensive taste for good living as mentioned. I recall, I went with her to see some houses in the area. As soon as she saw the house on Mount Bolus Road in Chapel Hill, she said, "Daddy, I want this house." So we purchased it, a few months before Vani and her family had actually moved to Chapel Hill. Vani and Murali still live there. They had since made many improvements and some attractive additions. I happen to have a special attachment with this house because I was involved in the renovation of the building, while Vani was doing a fellowship at Mayo Clinic in far-away Minnesota state.

7

Brief Stint in NTR's Government

WHENEVER I WAS IN INDIA, I usually stopped by in Hyderabad and visited N.T. Rama Rao, whether he was in power or not. We became very close friends and grew very fond of each other. It so happened that I was in India to attend a conference at Kovalam in Kerala in early 1996, where there were 100 experts in Indian studies – fifty from India and fifty from other countries. I along with Arvind Sharma were the two Indians who were invited to the Kovalam conference convened by Prof. K.S. Murty at the behest of Shri P.V. Narasimha Rao, then Prime Minister of India. On my way to the conference I met NTR in Hyderabad as usual before leaving for Kovalam. NTR asked me when I would return. I told him that I would come back a week later. He asked me to return a day earlier than I was planning and be with him to watch the election results as they came in. The elections for the State Assembly were underway. So I returned to Hyderabad and we watched the results on the TV. NTR received overwhelming support from the people with a clear verdict in his favor.

I congratulated NTR and told him that I would be leaving Hyderabad the next day. He said, "No, you should stay a little longer and be here during the time of my swearing in." So, I stayed back and settled in a room at Viceroy Hotel, close to the Tank Bund. There was a beeline of people visiting me, aspiring for all kinds of positions in the new government because they knew about my close relationship with NTR. These included even people aspiring for the chief secretary position, which was the top job for a bureaucrat. I made sure that none of these persons was accommodated. We chose as chief secretary Shri Rajaji, who never approached me or sent anyone to canvass on his behalf.

Next morning after the swearing in ceremony, I went to see NTR at his residence. We had breakfast together. Then, he asked me to drive with him in his official car to the Secretariat. I went along with him to the chief minister's office. NTR called the then Secretary of Education by name Rama Rao, who was there earlier also. NTR said to him? "you recall that Ramakrishna garu during his last visit told us that he would return to India for good and work for our government. Now he is here. What is the most suitable position that we could offer him?" I was totally surprised and bewildered; did not know what to say. The secretary asked him whether I would be advising him on educational policies or a general adviser on all matters. Without any hesitation, NTR said that I would be his advisor on all matters. The secretary said: "then he should be the Deputy Chairman of the A.P. Planning Board of which the Chief Minister is the Chairman." NTR responded: "What? Deputy

Chairman, no Vice-Chairman." There was no such position; it had to be created.

I told NTR that I had to go back to USA, where my wife and children lived, and settle all matters to felicitate my return to India for good. I needed at least a month's time to do this. NTR said that it was all fine, I could take leave for a month; but I should first join. I had no choice; signed the necessary papers and went back to USA. I quickly sold my house, hired a container, and loaded all my belongings including our Mercedes car and a lot of furniture. I still have most of these items, including the car at my residence in Visakhapatnam.

As I go through the newspaper clippings saved for me by my then personal secretary in two bound volumes, I recall how I was virtually behind the running of the Government of Andhra Pradesh. I say this at the cost of being misunderstood as going on an ego trip. We took three major decisions. One was the introduction of the Rs. 2 per kg rice scheme; so that rice reached the poorest of poor at a price they could afford. Second, we prohibited the sale of all kinds of alcoholic beverages. It was the poor people who were most adversely affected by consumption of alcohol. These two measures hit the state treasury very badly. However, the government was fully committed to implement them and find other means to overcome the revenue deficit. I am glad that the Government of Andhra Pradesh with Chandra Babu Naidu as the Chief Minister had introduced the program of Anna Canteens, serving a full meal at a meager cost of Rs.

5. This in some ways was a welcome extension of the Rs. 2 per kg rice scheme. The Anna Canteens were indeed a genuine tribute to NTR and his commitment to the poor.

The third policy decision was that the government should go to people and not vice versa. So we devised plans and programs to reach out to people and learn about their grievances, and address them then and there, when possible. I charted out a program that involved the chief minister and other major functionaries of the Andhra Pradesh government who would visit each district and interact directly with people to know first hand about their problems. I also instructed the officials in the secretariat and the districts to prepare perspective plans for each district pointing out the available assets, the liabilities faced, and the steps the government needed to take to exploit the full potential of available resources and provide for further development of the district. A hefty volume for each district was prepared.

The first phase of the projected program was a visit to Srikakulam, Vizianagaram, and Visakhapatnam districts, and then to take a break and return to Hyderabad before taking up the next phase to cover three more districts. We first visited Srikakulam; there was a tremendous response. We were in Garividi at a special cottage provided for us by Sreerama Corporation involved in ferro-alloys business.

At this point, we may note that N.T. Rama Rao had by then married Lakshmi Parvathi. The circumstances leading to this marriage deserve a mention. Some of these were shared with me by NTR himself. After NTR lost power, he was living in a small house belonging to one of his daughters. By then, he distributed most of his assets to his children. He was out of power, alone and lonely; something he could not handle. At that time, Lakshmi Parvathi, a Harikatha artist, approached him on the pretext of writing his biography. One day, when he was with her, NTR got a mild stroke. Lakshmi Parvathi rushed him to a hospital and implanted in his mind that she saved his life. Saying so repeatedly, she won NTR's life-time loyalty.

Lakshmi Parvathi accompanied NTR during these visits to the districts we undertook. It was no secret that Lakshmi Parvathi had ambitions beyond being wife of the chief minister. She wanted to run the government from behind.

After completing the visit to Srikakulam and Vizianagaram, we were on our way to Visakhapatnam. I received a call from highly informed people in Hyderabad. I learnt that when we were involved in our attempts to take the government to people, there were concerted efforts by Chandra Babu Naidu and his coterie to contact the MLAs and organize a coupe to unseat NTR, his father-in-law from the chief minister's position. I and others close to NTR were blissfully ignorant of all this. The dice were already cast against NTR. The majority of MLAs were no longer with him. Would NTR resign when he was told by his friends and well-wishers that he lost the support of majority in the legislature?

Dr. Jayaprakash Narayan, a bureaucrat with political interests, bold and forthright in his advice, and spotless in his character, who now heads the Lok Satta Party, was NTR's secretary. Jayaprakash asked me to go along with him to see NTR around 9:00 p.m. This was the hour when no one dared to disturb NTR, who usually went to bed early. I followed him. Jayaprakash told NTR that his government was likely to fall when the state assembly meets tomorrow. However, there was a chance to save his government, if he would issue a public statement saying that his wife Lakshmi Parvathi would be confined to home and would not interfere with the functioning of the government. NTR was visibly upset and angry. He looked at me, and I did not go to his support. He kicked the chair in front of him and said, in his dramatic style, "for want of this dirty chair, you want me to dishonor my wife. Go, and get lost. I would never make such a statement." We told to ourselves, NTR was willing to dishonor the verdict of millions of people in favor of his not so honorable wife. There was very little we could do, when NTR thus foreclosed all options to save his government. My personal loyalty to NTR prevented me, however, from taking the reasonable course of action and quit the government.

The coupe led by Chandra Babu Naidu was prompted by the fear that NTR, who had his eyes on becoming Prime Minister of India, now guided by Lakshmi Parvathi, might indeed move to Delhi.

NTR was the head of the united opposition. There was good chance that he might indeed succeed. If this really happened, Chandra Babu and his followers feared that Lakshmi Parvathi would take over as the head of the Telugu Desam Party (TDP) with ambition to become the next chief minister of the state. That would have been a disaster for the party and the state. Babu rose to the occasion and indeed saved the TDP and in a significant sense the State of Andhra Pradesh, even though those of us loyal to NTR despised it at that time. It was quite apparent that NTR would lose the confidence vote in the Assembly; and he was so informed by several of his close associates. However, NTR was reluctant to resign. He wanted to face the Assembly and see how all those MLAs whom he had handpicked and helped to win would vote against him.

NTR was chairman of the National Front against the Government of India then headed by Smt. Indira Gandhi. The other leaders of the front included Deve Gowda, then the Chief Minister of Karnataka, and V.P. Singh from Uttar Pradesh. Deve Gowda sensed that I had a good rapport with NTR and that he would likely to listen to my advice. He called me aside and told me that it would be honorable for NTR to voluntarily resign rather than face the no trust motion in the Assembly. If he followed such a course of action, he, as the Chairman of the United Front, would be a formidable candidate for prime minister's position. Jyoti Basu was being projected to head the opposition; but he would like instead NTR to become the next prime minister of India.

Even Chandra Babu Naidu might support him. He persuaded me to talk to NTR and convince him to resign. As it happened, Deve Gowda became the next prime minister of India, a position for which he thought that NTR would be the most appropriate candidate. Following Deve Gowda's suggestion, which seemed very sensible, I persuaded NTR to resign. He finally relented; and I had with me his signed letter of resignation to be sent to the governor. Obviously, Lakshmi Parvathi did not relish this development.

To continue our narrative, after the usual breakfast, I went to my house in the ministers' quarters. No sooner than I reached home, I received a call from my personal assistant that NTR was ill and that he was admitted in the hospital. I rushed to the hospital and found NTR in the hospital bed. He was surrounded by a number of MLAs who were still supporting him. Lakshmi Parvathi was at his bed side. We should note that I had with me his signed letter of resignation. As I entered the hospital room, a number of MLAs loyal to him mobbed me and asked me not to forward NTR's resignation letter to the governor. They said, now that he was sick, there would be a sympathy wave and that the number of MLAs supporting him would dramatically increase as it happened earlier when Indira Gandhi dismissed NTR's government. I was not convinced; but assured them that I would withhold his resignation letter until NTR gets well and that I would then ask him again whether he had changed his mind. After a few minutes, NTR opened his eyes; and it looked to me that he was quite normal. I told him about the resignation letter he gave me earlier; and asked him, if I should withhold and not forward it to the governor, as suggested by his loyalist MLAs. We might recall that I had already convinced him that it was in his best interests to resign and not face the Assembly for a trust vote. NTR gave his consent to forward his resignation letter to the governor.

I told Dr. Jayaprakash Narayan that NTR's resignation letter could now be sent to the governor. So, this chapter in NTR's life came to an end. Shri Chandra Babu Naidu was sworn in as the chief minister. Next morning, I took my letter of resignation as the Vice-Chairman of the State Planning Board to Chandra Babu and personally handed it over to him. I told him that I had three requests. First, I might be allowed to stay in minister's quarters for a few more months. I wanted to be with NTR during those difficult months. Second, whatever little government furniture NTR had at his house should remain and not taken away. Vehicles were already waiting outside at NTR's residence to shift it. Third, we worked very hard to prepare a bill for the reorganization of school education in the state. It received appreciation from UNESCO experts. It was about to be introduced in the Assembly. Because of some extraneous interruptions we decided to withhold it for the next session. It was my considered opinion that it should be carried through in the coming session of the Assembly. Babu readily agreed for the first two. Regarding the third, he said that he could not accept because the teachers were opposed to it. I told him that it was something to be expected because as per the provisions in the new bill, parents of children enrolled in schools would have an important role to play in the management of the schools. Chandra Babu flatly said that he could not afford to alienate teachers at that point of time, when he was trying to stabilize his government.

I continued my stay in Hyderabad primarily to be with NTR at this difficult time. All kinds of people used to come to him and feed false hopes that he would soon become the chief minister. Now, in addition to experiencing natural depression on the turn of events, he had increasingly become delusional that he would be back in power. There was none around him who gave a frank and realistic assessment of the state of affairs. NTR sent his former Advocate General Shri Ramachandra Rao to Delhi for a meeting with Shri P.V. Narasimha Rao, the then prime minister of India, hoping that he would have support from Delhi. Ramachandra Rao on his return from Delhi first went to Chandra Babu Naidu and congratulated him before coming to see NTR. I was a helpless spectator. It was a hopeless situation.

So, I decided to leave for Visakhapatnam, my home town. Just a few days after that, I received the news that NTR passed away. I rushed to Hyderabad, and went to NTR's house, expecting that his body would be there. The front door was closed. I was received by NTR's trusted and loyal attendant Prasad and taken into the house through the back door. On my way in, I found a group of journalists who interrupted and told me about the events that were taking place inside. They wondered if I came to get my share. I told them quite rudely to "shut up" and to mind their own business. However, I was shocked to see in the house people including some of NTR's children guarding the "strong" room where NTR kept his valuables.

NTR's body was already shifted to Lal Bahadur Stadium. So, I went there to pay my last respects. As I entered the stadium, I found Chandra Babu Naidu and some of his followers in one room and NTR's loyalist MLAs in another room. I saw Babu in his room and told him, now that NTR was gone there could be only one Telugu Desam Party and that the time had come to unite all factions. Babu appeared very agreeable to this idea.

Next morning, there was a meeting of NTR loyalist MLAs at his residence. I attended the meeting. I was asked to speak first. I told the group that I met Babu earlier and that he was in a mood to reconcile. I can negotiate a fair deal so that some of them may be accommodated in the government as ministers. This suggestion did not go well with the majority of the people in the room. One of them said, "Let Babu first resign, then we talk about reconciliation." I told him, "Why would Babu resign? It is unreasonable to expect that. It is now a very opportune time for them to negotiate for a few berths in the cabinet."

Apparently, they felt that the sympathy wave generated by NTR's demise would favor them and that there would be a general revolt against Chandra Babu

Naidu. They were very unrealistic. If they heeded to my advice, some of them would have been in the government in charge of some important portfolios. Actually, one of them Shri Prasanna Kumar Reddy told me later that they made a big mistake by not taking my advice seriously. As it happened, the so-called NTR loyalist MLAs gradually drifted one after another into Babu's camp less gracefully.

8

Beginning of a New Phase

WITH NTR GONE, I had little interest in politics or playing any role in public life. I returned to my home town Visakhapatnam and began to think about how I may get back to pursue my academic interests. One option was to return to USA and teach at one of the universities. Another was to start my own establishment in Visakhapatnam. Of course, these were not mutually exclusive. I could do both. That was how the Institute for Human Science and Service came into being. I gave a house owned by my family with its over 10,000 sq. ft plinth area to locate the institute. It functioned there until we moved it into GITAM University, where it was merged with what is now named as the School of Gandhian Studies.

Returning to Visakhapatnam and the new initiatives I had undertaken were a kind of academic rebirth for me. During the later part of my stay at the Institute of Parapsychology in USA and the brief period in the Andhra Pradesh government, I was more an administrator with little time to pursue my own academic work. My larger agenda of pursuing consciousness studies, to provide a reasonable theoretical base for parapsychological findings, and to build a viable model for understanding human nature as a composite of natural and paranormal functions, remained largely unfulfilled. I felt that the time had come to return to my academic pursuits and leave behind the extraneous responsibilities, which might be more glamorous to look at from public perspective, but in reality lacked real substance and personal meaning in the long run.

So, it would seem, destiny determined once again the course of my life, opening up wide horizons to explore new frontiers of knowledge. As it would become more clear as we move on to narrate the rest of the story, I was fortunate to enjoy good health – physically, mentally, and emotionally – and continue at the age of 86 to be intellectually productive and physically active. I attend my office at GITAM regularly on all working days, and go swimming or walking almost every evening at the century-old Waltair Club. During my 85th year, I am privileged to publish five books. It is truly satisfying to write the book *Gandhi's Dharma*, published by Oxford University Press. Gandhi has been an inspiration almost from my school days. I firmly believe that Gandhi's *yoga* of nonviolence is the only hope for bringing perennial peace to humankind.

Back in Visakhapatnam, I began functioning from home, enjoying the freedom of movement and not being tied down to a preset agenda. I did not need to keep regular office hours, I shuttled back and forth between USA and India. All my children were already settled in the US. First, I took a brief assignment to teach at the University of Tennessee, Chattanooga Campus, staying with my daughter Rani. Then I moved on to the University of North Carolina, Chapel Hill. Living with my daughter Vani, I taught there courses on "Consciousness: East and West." My book *Consciousness Studies* (2002) is an outcome of these teaching assignments.

All this was not without its costs in some other ways. I lost great opportunity to strengthen my financial base in India. Before my visit to USA, I was much into real estate investments. It was the best time to buy land for development. I had funds to make major purchases. I did not take advantage of the available opportunities, because of my trips to USA. If I did, I would have been one of the richest guys in our circle of family and friends. However, I have no regrets. Money had never been a main concern; and I am comfortably provided with enough funds to meet my needs. Too much money has its own handicaps; it tends to become an end in itself, rather than a means to achieve loftier goals.

As mentioned, Vani and Murali moved to Chapel Hill leaving the palacious home they built in Madisonville, primarily because Sarojini and I were in Durham. In a way, by returning to India, we had let them down.

To get back to our narrative, Vani wanted to remodel her house in Chapel Hill, and add a few more rooms. However, she was doing a fellowship in neurology at the Mayo Clinic, known to be one of the best in the world, the place where presidents and princess went for treatment. At that time, my son with his wife Madhu was living in Cary, close to Chapel Hill. Since I had free time on hand, staying with my son, I chose to supervise the remodeling of Vani's house. I have a lot of memories of rebuilding the house. For example, Vani wanted a special kind of staircase built. It was not easy to find a person around who could do it. I had to do a lot of search before finding one. Vani chose to add a few more rooms on the third floor to be newly built. The previous main floor was totally redone. All the earlier bedrooms on that floor were converted into one large bedroom with a huge dressing room and a modern attached bath with German fittings specially ordered. Whenever I am in Chapel Hill, Vani puts me up in that room with a large working desk and an Apple computer with windows on south and west sides, giving a great look at the beautiful landscape.

More than a year went by before I could get back to my academic work. During 2003, I published literally nothing. Then I bounced back and my academic work in one form or another continues without interruption.

The focus of my academic interest shifted, however, from parapsychology to Indian psychology and its spiritual aspects. The contrast of science and spirituality as two inherently conflicting approaches appeared spurious and untenable. It has been a challenge to find the appropriate bridges to connect the two realms. Indian psychology increasingly seemed to me to be the discipline best suited for that purpose.

I edited along with Sonali Bhatt Marwaha the book *Towards a Spiritual Psychology* published in 2005. It was the beginning of the continuing journey to find the true "spirit" behind driving human nature. My interest in Mahatma Gandhi was further strengthened by Gandhi's conception of human nature as a composite of the animal and the human. The human, it would seem, is man's spiritual side.

The interest in Indian psychology led me to focus attention on its relevance to the current areas of interest like cognition. At an international conference on cognitive science held at the University of Allahabad, I pleaded for promoting indigenous cognitive science. While returning from Allahabad on a flight to Delhi I happened to sit next to Dr. Murali Manohar Joshi, a physicist with much interest in *yoga* and Indian psychology, who was then the Union Minister of Education. That gave us an opportunity to discuss ways of promoting Indian psychology as a discipline of study in Indian colleges and universities. We shared common interest in *yoga* and its significance to humankind, not merely as a tool for physical health but also as a way for spiritual development. Regrettably, he was not in power for too long after that to implement some of the ideas we shared.

During the next several years, my focus was mainly on Indian psychology and consciousness studies, which seem to go together in many ways. I had attempted to formulate a long series of principles behind Indian psychology and how Indian psychology offers a viable, alternative paradigm to guide psychology in general. I had the occasion to present these ideas in several conferences around the world, for example, first at the Indiana State University and later at the 17th International Congress of Vedanta at Miami University, Oxford, Ohio. The final outcome is the development of Trisula or BMC Model of the person where I attempt to show the relative places of body, mind, and consciousness (spirit) in human functioning.

In addition to the attempts to connect science and spirituality, and to reconcile Eastern and Western perspectives on consciousness, I tried to explore the possibilities of applying the tenants of Indian psychology to education, health, and wellness. The culmination of this effort is my book *Foundations of Yoga Psychology* (2017). Thirty-six years ago, I envisaged the relevance of *yoga* for enhancing human potentials and helped to establish the Yoga Village as a part of Andhra University, when I headed it. Therefore, it is truly satisfying that *yoga* is now internationally recognized as a helpful discipline to practice and study and that the United Nations designated June 21st as International Day of Yoga. Prime Minister Shri Narendra Modi deserves all the credit for truly putting *yoga* on the global stage. Therefore, I dedicated to him my recent book *Patanjali's Yogasutra: A Psychological Study* (2018).

I have also attempted to draw the contours of Indian psychology from different perspectives such as Advaita and Buddhist schools of Indian thought. Along with Anand Paranjpe and A.K. Dalal, I edited the volume *Handbook of Indian Psychology* published by Cambridge University Press (2008). Another edited volume is *Yoga and Parapsychology* (2010), which calls attention to the fact that the basic gourd on which parapsychology can be firmly built in *yoga* as described in Patanjali's *yogasutra.*

The culmination of my efforts to place Indian psychology on the world map is the joint effort with my academic twin brother Dr. Anand Paranjpe. The book *Psychology in the Indian Tradition* (Rao and Paranjpe 2016) is the main product coming out of this collaboration.

Started with interest in Indian thought, but strayed into other areas and stayed there for a greater part of my professional career, I am finally succeeded in finding my roots. I authored the book *Foundations of Yoga Psychology* (2017). My most recent exercise is *Srimad Bhagavadgita: A Treatise on Counselling* (2018).

At this time, my interest in Mahatma Gandhi has become more pronounced and intense. His philosophy and practices appear to be more relevant to humankind now than during his own lifetime. So, I am currently engaged not merely in studying and writing on Gandhi, but more importantly finding ways of more effectively promoting Gandhi's *yoga* of nonviolence. The forthcoming 150th birth anniversary of Mahatma offers an excellent opportunity to call the attention of the world to the peril of the strife-torn, conflict-filled, and terror-driven human predicament of the time and the need to move on the path the Mahatma had laid for us decades ago to make this world a more livable place, and less prone for self-destruction.

History made us to become painfully aware that violence outlived its utility as a useful instrument of conflict resolution; and has become obsolete as a survival mechanism. Yet, violence is rampant in our societies; and is widely practiced as a natural mode of response to conflicts of all kinds. The progress of science and benefits of technology, one fears, may become a burden rather than a boon to humankind, if the physical developments are not accompanied by necessary moral support. Material abundance and moral bankruptcy cannot coexist without devastating effects on the planet.

Gandhiji's thought and practices were centered around the paradox of material abundance and moral bankruptcy. He had the courage and conviction to explicitly denounce material progress without the attendant moral balancing. He saw clearly that the humankind was heading on a destructive path and that we need to retrace our steps to bring balance and harmony between the material longings and moral compulsions. In other words, he found the asymmetry in the progress of physical science and technology on one side and the human science and moral development on the other as particularly frightening. He felt an urgent need to bring about a balance between them. In addressing this issue, he formulated a comprehensive theoretical framework with important implications for human science, economic practices, and political governance, and for pursuing science and building character. His thought provides a rational base and the spiritual hope of freeing all from hunger, disease, discrimination, and deprivation, and at the same time helping to liberate the inner spirit to assert itself, manifesting its divine, altruist nature.

Mahatma Gandhi sought to reform education from ground level. Good education relevant to our real needs is a necessary condition for progress. He said that our universities make our students foreigners in their own country. We celebrated our 70th Independence Day. Yet, we still have the colonial system of education, ignoring our rich legacy from very ancient times, and great aptitude to learn and discover truth. The Mahatma focused on three aspects of education – character building, personality development, and learning skills to serve the society. His craft-centered education is an attempt to achieve this, and it is consistent with Indian ethos and values.

Indian education has a hoary history. It embodies not merely Indian culture; it is indeed its culture. This was the case with what is considered now ancient system of education, which lasted until the beginning of thirteenth century CE somewhat eclipsed during medieval period and the Mogul rule. Indian education lost its native moorings completely during the British colonial rule. The education we now have in India is essentially a colonial transplant, significantly different from the classical system of Indian education as well as education in India during the Islamic rule.

During the pre-Buddhist period, education was not institutionalized. There were no organized schools and colleges. It was imparted by individual teachers. It was entirely a private affair and not a public provision. However, teaching was part of the duties of a class of people known as brahmanas (brahmins). It was combined with religion. Thus, what we had during the period is religious education imparted to individuals privately by individual teachers. However, there were forums where one could show and test his learning, and receive recognition.

With the advent of Buddhism, education tended to be institutionalized. Educational institutions arose out of Buddhist monasteries. We find their culmination in the institutions like Nalanda University. It is not the case that there were no centers of higher learning prior to the advent of Buddhism. Indeed Takshashila and Benares were thriving centers of high-class education. There were, however, no colleges or universities located in them. Teacher himself was an institution. Students in search of higher education flocked around renowned teachers.

Indian tradition from the Vedic times emphasized the importance of character. The *Manusmriti* asserts that a man of character is to be preferred to one with knowledge of the Vedas but lacks purity in thought and practice. Visitors from different countries at different times, belonging to different faiths, from Megasthenes to Marco Polo, uniformly had nothing but praise for the character of Indians. For example, here is a quote from Yuan Chwang of seventh century CE, an objective and critical observer. He said referring to Indians:

> They are of hasty and irresolute temperament but of *pure moral principles*. They will not take anything wrongfully and they yield more than fairness requires. They fear for retribution for sins in other lives and make light of what conduct produces in this life. *They do not practice deceit and they keep their sworn obligations.*

Along with character building, personality development was a major aim of education in ancient India. The training of the student as a *brahmacharin* with an emphasis on cultivating self-control, self-respect, and self-reliance is a case in point. Simplicity of life and habits were prized virtues. Voluntary poverty was not an uncommon practice of those engaged in higher education. The value of non-possession bestows unlimited freedom on the person. Self-control is the key here. Simplicity of life involves both self-respect and self-assertion. It tames the ego; and at the same time it enhances one's self-esteem.

Ancient Indian system of education also stressed the importance of social responsibilities and civic duties. Do your duty as a citizen was the dictum. Each profession had its code of honor, which invariably emphasized the social responsibilities.

With the Muslim invasion and European colonization these aims and values were given a go-by. The Indian mindset has come to play a second fiddle. Education became merely a tool to serve the rulers. The kind of education we have is a colonial transplant. Our universities are attempted replicas of institutions functioning in other countries and cultures, far removed from native ethos. We still suffer from what I call the "colonial syndrome." We imitate and value other cultures and neglect our own.

Consequently, we continue to suffer from colonial remnants. However, we are hoping to correct the situation by emphasizing Gandhian values and embracing his aims of education. Along with developing skills and acquiring knowledge, we stress character building and personality development of our students. We do not share the view that secular education does not subscribe to a set of values or that science is value-free. Education devoid of values is no education. Science without values is worse than useless; it can be dangerous. What we do and say here is that we must attempt to implement Mahatma is ideas on education, suitably adapting them to the current state of the country.

Peace and War

Peace is something we all desire. It is generally considered as what comes after conflict. Today with the widespread availability of weapons of mass destruction, peace may not be conceived as something that follows war. For there would be no victors left to enjoy peace after the war. People from all sides would be victims of self-destruction. Therefore, peace should be considered on its own without reference to war, as a condition to prevent conflicts and consequent wars and not as a state that follows a war.

The common expression is War and Peace. *War and Peace* is a classic novel by Leo Tolstoy. The central message of the novel is that people change. Conflict comes first; and peace follows unrest. I have deliberately chosen to reverse the order because I think there is an urgent need to accord priority to peace without reference to conflict. Peace need not be conceived as something that follows war, but a state prior to war that pre-empts, as it were, the very possibility of war. The shift of emphasis from war to peace is an urgent necessity because the available weapons of mass destruction, if unleashed, would leave no one behind to experience peace.

It is observed that war is as old as humankind; but peace is a modern invention (Howard 2000). This is a Western perspective. In the native Indian tradition, the quest for peace is as old as waging war. It is in the nature of human mind that it wavers and wanders. Consequently, it is conflict-prone, and harbors seeds of unrest. Wars, therefore, are natural phenomena. They are endemic to mankind and ubiquitous in human history. Peace on the other hand is not a fact of daily life. Rather it is an elusive goal to be achieved. Secure peace is a mirage in the desert sands of daily living. However, peace in the long Indian tradition is something desired, a goal strived for, and a state sought to be cultivated for wholesome living. The German philosopher Immanuel Kant had advanced a similar view much later.

Wars originate, as it is often observed, in the minds of men. The approach to seeking peace lies then in controlling the conflict-proneness of the mind; making it steady and steadfast, which may be accomplished by cultivating a state of focused attention with peace as the goal. This fact was recognized in the Indian tradition since antiquity. Patanjali's *Yogasutra* explicitly addresses this issue. It states at the outset that the goal of *yoga* is to control the wandering mind and make it steady and focused.

Peace may be understood in a weak or strong sense. Weak peace involves mere absence of external conflicts. Strong peace is an enduring state of goodwill and comradeship. Nonviolence and peace are coextensive. They cover similar if not the same ground. Nonviolence like peace may be conceived in a strong or weak sense. In its strong sense, nonviolence is more than refraining from causing injury to others. It is a state of subjective experience of conflict-free stillness of mind and tranquility. Like nonviolence, violence and war have external and internal manifestations and ramifications. Violence breaks peace. Nonviolence restores peace. Violence is destructive; and nonviolence is constructive. Violence may bring external peace, only to be disturbed later, because violence breeds more violence. It is in the very nature of violence to perpetuate itself. In contrast, nonviolence not only brings peace, but it also sustains and spreads peace. War, if it brings any peace, would be peace in the weak sense with its external manifestation devoid of inner experience. Strong nonviolence, however, promotes peace in its strong sense. Methods of enforcing peace by violence, as in the case of war, do little to promote inner peace. Suppressing overt conflict is insufficient to generate inner peace, which may be cultivated only by mental discipline. Nonviolence radiates peace; violence churns unrest in the mind and disturbs inner peace. Nonviolence and peace in their strong sense embody goodwill and self-sacrifice. Nonviolence entails love. Love is the secret of the art of good and peaceful living.

Concept of Peace

In the Indian tradition, peace is the most cherished goal of human endeavor. Many rituals include the chanting of the peace *mantra*: peace, peace, and peace be unto all (*shanti, shanti, shantih*). As mentioned, like nonviolence, peace may be weak or strong. Peace in the weak sense refers to absence of external conflicts and hostilities. In its strong sense, peace is more than absence of external conflicts; it is an inner experience. It is an enduring state of goodwill and comradeship, personal and subjective. In the *Yajurveda*, we find "May everything in the universe be at peace. Let peace pervade everywhere, at all times. May I experience that peace within my own heart" (Max Müller 1884/1995, *The Upanishads*, part II, *Yajurveda*, 36: 17, Oxford: Clarendon Press). This passage refers to both the senses of peace and how they are interrelated. It is a holistic conception of peace.

In Buddhist tradition, peace is the end of suffering, achieved by the control of all cravings.

Desires create an endless cycle of action and reaction, birth and death. In the cessation of such desires one finds peace. Nonviolence is the most cherished virtue in the Jain tradition. Injury or harm to any living being is considered sinful.

The Christian Gospel (Matthew 5.9) also preaches peace. Cultivating peace is the way to the Kingdom of God. Christian Fathers since the time of St. Augustine were pacifists.

Peace may be physical, psychological, or spiritual. Physical peace refers to a state of rest and relaxation of the body. Mental peace is a stress-free state, and consists in one's experience of stillness and tranquility. Spiritual peace involves a state of serenity, bliss, and self-perpetuating happiness (*ananda*).

The three aspects of peace are interrelated. Relaxed body helps to promote mental peace. Mental peace is a prelude to spiritual peace. We find this amply illustrated in Yoga literature.

In this context, we may ask: What is the relation between experience of peace within oneself and the peace we find among the members of a community and between communities, between one state and others? It goes without saying that peace in the society is conducive for peace to prevail in the person. However, the question arises as to how the peace-experience in the person promotes societal peace? What is the relation between the two kinds of peace – external and internal – if we may so label them? External peace, as mentioned, is peace in the weak sense. It connotes simply absence of overt conflict. Internal peace involves actual experience of peace by the person. Internal peace is cultivated by wholesome conduct. Wholesome conduct is behavior where the person is utterly detached and egoless. He is free from hatred and delusion. Such behavior presupposes goodwill and altruism.

An experience of wholesome behavior implies wholesome interaction with others surrounding him. Wholesome conduct is ethically driven and guided. This involves establishing a reciprocal relationship between self and others. Such a relationship becomes reflexive and reflective in that the individual and the society mirror each other and reinforce each other. There is thus a nexus between individual and society; and between inner and outer peace.

It is not possible to experience peace with mere exercise of reason alone. Reason is at the root of personal identities. Hence it is in a sense inconsistent with the notion of inherent unity among all humans, even if reason suggests the desirability of such unity. Reason, therefore, may not be considered a sufficient factor for promoting unity and harmony among people. There are limits to what reason could achieve. Here comes spirituality as the crucial binding factor. Spiritual in this context does not refer to the other-worldly or a transcendent order. To be spiritual is to go beyond self. It involves reaching out to others, extending self to include others.

Again, peace is more than mental peace. The aforesaid nexus between individual and society, inasmuch as it involves egolessness and altruism, takes on a spiritual dimension. To be spiritual is to transcend the ego. Altruism is a spiritual virtue. In a spiritual state, there is harmony between peace within and peace in the world. In the Indian tradition, the peace within radiates and reaches outside. As the *Yogasutra* clearly states, in the presence of one who is nonviolent, others become nonviolent. Mahatma Gandhi's life is a contemporary example.

While conflict, combat, and war are instinctive to humankind, because they are inherent in the very nature of the mind, which is conflict-prone, the desire for and pursuit of peace are things to be cultivated. They are, however, widely present for millennia in world history.

In early times in China, a scholar and a gentleman were more respected and honored than a soldier and military personnel. Peace and harmony were considered as more exalted states than political and military victories. In Confucius, the great Chinese thinker and moralist, Jen is the central ethical concept. He defines Jen in the following words:

> In public behave as you would in the presence of an honored guest. Set the people their proper tasks with as much care as if you were conducting a great sacrifice. The treatment you would not have for yourself, do not handout to other people.
>
> – quoted from Murty and Bouquet 1960, *Studies in the Problems of Peace*, p. 21 Bombay: Asia Publishing House

Following Confucius, Mencius (371–289 BCE) declared that there could be no righteous wars. Such an expression is a contradiction in terms. He asserted the inherent goodness of human beings and their innate wisdom to discriminate the right from the wrong. This implies that wisdom and ability to know and assert truth is not limited to a few but widely available to all people. This then is a natural resource which helps to prevent wars.

As is well known, Buddhism advocates commitment to absolute abandonment of all forms of violence. For the Buddha, universal love and nonviolence are central to the practice of the art of virtuous life. The very first principle of *panchsheel* is the vow of abstaining from causing harm to other living beings. Even earlier than Gautama, the Buddha, Vardhamana, another kshatriya coming from a warrior class, proclaimed the principle of *ahimsa* (nonviolence) which continues to influence the lives of many Jainas in India. What is relevant here is that the Buddha's influence went beyond his native land and had affected the lives of many millions of people in other parts of Asia. The urge for peace, the attitude of "peace-mindedness", and its advocacy by such people as Mahatma Gandhi in the twentieth century are a continuation of the Buddhist legacy and the classical Indian tradition.

Jawaharlal Nehru, whom Gandhi designated as his heir, borrowed the concept *panchsheel*; and he was explicit in his commitment to it. We may recall that the *panchsheel*, as outlined by the Buddha includes the following commandments:

1. refrain from injuring other living beings,
2. refrain from taking what does not belong,
3. refrain from sexual misconduct,
4. refrain from telling a lie, and
5. refrain from consuming intoxicants such as liquor.

Nehru applied *panchsheel* in his engagement and treaties with other nations, such as China. He stated the *panchsheel* principles as follows:

1. respect for sovereignty and territorial integrity of other states,
2. non-aggression,
3. non-interference in the internal affairs of other nations,
4. observing the principle of equality for mutual benefit, and
5. peaceful coexistence between states.

The above are Nehru's rendering of *panchsheel* as principles to be followed in preparing the policies of the state rather than as guidelines for one's personal conduct. In other words, Nehru recognized and asserted *panchsheel* to be more than personal virtues, and wished to practice them as an explicit policy of the state. In Nehru, we thus find the application of *panchsheel* to statecraft.

Ashoka, the celebrated Indian king, made a willful commitment for spreading the message of peace and love. In his illustrious career, we find an exemplary case of transition from upholding the view that violence and war are unavoidable even for a well-meaning, peace-minded noble king to a belief that nonviolence is a necessary virtue to practice even for a king. We learn from rock edicts he left behind that sounds of war should be replaced by proclamation of *ahimsa* as the *dharma*. As we know, Ashoka conquered Kalinga. However, he repented and felt that a loss of "even a thousandth part of all lives that were killed or died or carried away captive at the time when Kalinga was conquered" was deplorable (Rock Edict XIII). The edict further notes that Ashoka considered "that even he who wrongs him is fit to be forgiven of wrongs that can be forgiven" (quoted from Murty and Bouquet 1960,*Studies in the Problems of Peace*. Bombay: Asia Publishing House, p. 29).

To take an example from the West, we may take the case of Alexander the Great, the Macedonian king of fourth century BCE. Alexander was a student of the great Greek philosopher Aristotle. Some see him as a blood-thirsty king bent on conquering the world. Some others find in him the merit of attempting to bring Europe and Asia together and create a world state. Yet, a few others credit him as a crusader to uphold the notion of the brotherhood of all human beings (Tarn 1948/1979, *Alexander the Great*, Cambridge: Cambridge University Press). As Bouquet notes, drawing from Tarn, the culmination point of Alexander the Great is the banquet held for 9,000 guests, where Alexander had at his table representatives of other nations that included among others Macedonians, Persian, and Greeks. Referring to Alexander's prayer at this dinner, which took place one year before his death, Bouquet notes:

> It seems luminously clear from all this that Alexander was praying for something like world-peace and fellowship, and for harmony between Europeans and Asians, representatives of whom he had at his table, and whom he wished to regard one another as brothers.
> – Murty and Bouquet 1960, *Studies in the Problems of Peace*. Bombay: Asia Publishing House.33

There are three generally recognized basic theories of peace (Howard, M. 2009a. "Preface: Concluding Peace", in Williamson Murray and Jim Lacey (eds) *The Making of Peace: Rulers, States, and the Aftermath of War*. Cambridge: Cambridge University Press.). One theory equates peace with the absence of war. Thomas Hobbes is one of those who advocate this view. The second theory upholds peace as the prevalence of "just order" in society. St. Augustine has proclaimed such a view. Just order may be seen as something divinely ordained or in current times as the one that has popular endorsement. The third theory considers peace as something not given or bestowed by divine will or the state but a condition that should be created, promoted, and maintained by constant human effort. Immanuel Kant is an important champion of such a view.

Making Peace

Now, we may raise the question how we may make

and maintain peace. Violence and war as means of achieving peace are inherently flawed. The reason is very simple. Two contraries cannot coexist in life without causing conflict sooner or later. Peace and war are like light and darkness. They are mutually exclusive. One may politically/physically subdue another person/state by force of violence. It will not make either the conqueror or the conquered virtuous and keep neither at peace. It looks as though that this fact was realized by Ashoka at the end of the Kalinga War and by Alexander the Great toward the end of his life. Mahatma Gandhi asserted its continued relevance to contemporary world conditions.

With weapons of mass destruction made available even to small countries ruled by apparently not very stable and humane persons, as we sense in North Korea, it is obvious that nonviolence at the individual as well as at the state level is the only viable alternative for war and destruction. Any violent attempts to contain violence tend to be self-destructive. This is one of the reasons behind the notion that balance of power is a means of maintaining peace. Such, however, is a precarious proposition. Today, we have in place numerous alliances and treaties and of course the overarching United Nations with the explicit goal of making and maintaining peace between nations. Yet, outbreaks of wars in various parts of the world are not an uncommon phenomenon. It follows that any physically driven force, however well meant, is insufficient to bring about sustaining peace even externally, let alone generating internal peace.

Now, what may we do for peace to prevail on the planet. Is there any viable alternative to physical force for making and maintaining peace? We believe there is. Pursuit of strong peace is the alternative. Strong peace is inner driven and ethically guided. Violence in any form is ruled out as a tool to secure peace. Peace in the strong sense is peace secured and sustained by nonviolence. Here we may draw from Mahatma Gandhi and the native Indian tradition. The underlying assumption is that inner peace is reflexive of external peace. Inner peace promotes outer peace as nothing else does.

Cultivating inner peace calls for self-discipline, and developing the culture of extending self to include others. It involves attempts to eliminate the ego, to reduce oneself to a zero in the words of Mahatma Gandhi. The vacuum generated by emptying the mind of the ego will be filled by the emerging values of love and altruism. One is then truly led into the spiritual realm.

It is not enough, we make peace. We should endeavor with equal zeal to maintain peace with the goal of achieving perpetual peace. Permanent peace is possible only with spreading inner peace to encompass the entire humankind. For this we need more than media and parental support to generate the peace-attitude. It calls for actual experience of peace within. This is possible in the Indian tradition by practice of *yoga*, focused attention, and meditation on peace.

All this sounds well, one may say, and ask whether

it is realistic to expect this to happen in the real world we live in. It is a legitimate question; but then look at the current state of affairs – availability of weapons of mass destruction to even small countries like North Korea ruled by men blinded by unrealistic ambitions and total disregard for international obligations. Do we have really a choice? There seems to be no alternative to awakening grassroots awareness of virtues of nonviolence and the need to eliminate violence in all its forms. One may wonder whether there is sufficient time to pull the world back from the precipice of self-destruction precipitated by war by the slow process of awakening grassroots awareness. Yet, there seems to be no choice except to hope that the efficacy of nonviolence as an instrument of peace is in the realm of the possible. This is the only hope for the continued survival of humankind. Any pessimism in this regard would only spell an inevitable doom for the entire world. Perpetual peace would remain a pipe dream of a few philosophers.

Now what can we do as parents, teachers, and statesmen to help our children to cultivate the attitude of "peace-mindedness"? Children are exposed day in and day out to scenes of violence. They learn from episodes of entertainment that violence conquers evil and promotes our well-being. They are hardly ever told stories of nonviolence that are more effective and lasting as instruments to banish evil and promote love and well-being, and that nonviolence calls for as much valour and courage as any form of violence.

The media have a role to play. They should desist

from sensationalizing violence, and depict instead nonviolence not as a sedate state but an active force, physically efficacious, morally warranted, and spiritually satisfying. Children should be made aware of the virtues of nonviolence at a very early age by their parents and teachers. The books they read in school should expressly devote themselves to promote "peace-mindedness" and commitment to nonviolence as a personal and social virtue. They should be exposed to the lives of Vardhamana, Gautama Buddha, Ashoka, and Mahatma Gandhi and similar others like Albert Schweitzer, Martin Luther King, and Nelson Mandela, depicting them as role models, heroes to emulate, and pious people to inspire. The sooner we begin to do this, the safer would be the planet from the catastrophe staring at us.

What does Gandhi mean for the younger generation, for the future of our country? Gandhi is a formidable combination of idealism and pragmatism. For the youth of today, Gandhi stands for the practical approach that can enable them to apply values and ethics in every sphere of life. Gandhi stands for the all-inclusive vision of development where our smart cities grow together with smart villages and smarter agricultural farms. Gandhi symbolizes the quest for that truth and nonviolence which shall liberate us by helping us to discover ourselves in the selfless service of others. For the youth of today, Gandhi is the voice that continually reminds them that there is no religion greater than the religion of humanity. And today, when we live in a world where we have the most sophisticated weapons and the constant shadow of bloodshed and terrorism, we need to listen to the voice of the Mahatma more than ever before.

India from its antiquity is a land conspicuous with its philosophical outlook. It has been India's tradition to look beyond the existential situation and think about things more enduring than the passing. It was not the past and the history of what had gone by that became the subject of main concern but the future where one would go, the goals to be achieved, the methods to be adopted, and the guideposts to look for in the process. Thus, what is truly a sustaining force behind Indian philosophical inquiry is the search for the permanent and eternal, and not the ephemeral and the changing. It is the relentless and diligent search for the main supporting substratum underlying all change that interested Indian thinkers from antiquity. The futuristic perspective is an indelible characteristic underlying the mainstream of Indian thought. However, the future is seen embedded in the present. It is holographic. In a sense, it is an interesting conception of "eternal present," which may be seen as dispensing with the category of time. This might look like a paradox; but the resolution of such seeming incongruities had been a challenge, which philosophers in India did not shy away from addressing.

While the goal of the search remains an ideal, the search itself is practical. *Yoga* stands for both the search and what is sought for. In this context, the goal to be achieved and the method of achieving become reflexive of each other. Means and ends thus become two faces of the same coin. Perhaps, a more appropriate analogy is that of the seed and the tree, like the acorn and the oak. *Yoga* may be seen as the seed as well as the tree of Indian philosophical tradition. The tradition involves more than the Hindu systems of thought, which no doubt are its main branches. The other branches include Buddhism, Jainism, and numerous other lesser known ones. *Yoga* has germinated and manifested in many distinct forms. Indeed, *yoga* is central and occupies a pivotal position in Indian way of life – in thought, passion, and action. It is integral, binding intellectual pursuits, emotional engagement, and daily activities in Indian way of life. Not only is *yoga* an index of Indian culture, it may also be seen as a mark of Indian identity.

The antecedents of *yoga* may be traced to wandering ascetics. These ascetics included people seeking pleasures as well as those who denounced them and deprived themselves of mundane sensuous gratification. Some scholars called them "wandering swarms of ascetics." Some writers described the yogic exercises of that time as "ecstatic rites of savages" (see Ramachandra Rao 1999). What we have come to know as Yoga system since the time of Patanjali (about 200 BCE) is what Patanjali by his own admission gleaned, edited, and systematized. *Yoga* did not originate with him. From all evidence, *yoga* and yogic practices predate the Vedic period. Patanjala *yoga* and various important commentaries following it such as those of Vyasa, Vachaspati, Vijnanabhikshu, and Bhoja, as

Ramachandra Rao notes, refer to the *yoga* "sanctified by the Vedic tradition" (1999: 5).

It would seem that *yoga* in antiquity was the general and accepted ascetic culture of the time. It was not theory loaded or theistically oriented. It was just a way of life, characterizing the people at the time. Such a conclusion may seem odd to those who have come to regard Yoga as a system of Hindu philosophy. However, the fact that *yoga* practices were not limited to Hindus and were part of the way of life of Buddhists and other non-theistic systems of thought needs to be taken serious note of, when we discuss *yoga*. It seems more reasonable to think that *yoga* is a native Indian culture not limited by or confined to any single system of philosophy.

If India has sponsored the United Nation's resolution to have an International Yoga Day, it does not imply that Yoga is trans-Indian in its origin. Rather it may be seen as being an extension of the Indian conception of *vasudhaiva kutumbakam* (the notion of universal brotherhood).

If Samkhya provided the theoretical/knowledge base of Indian culture, Yoga showed its practical applications in life. It is our contention that *yoga* is the seed, and that Indian thought and culture from antiquity to the present constitute the tree that grew out of it. What follows is an exploration of this theme. In a nutshell, the goal of human endeavor in Indian tradition is freedom. Yoga's goal is liberation; it is liberation from mental constraints. Yogic practices are the ways to achieve liberation. Thus *yoga* constitutes the goal as well as the means to achieve that goal.

Liberation is self-realization. Self-realization is discovering one's true self. In modern psychological terminology, it is self-actualization. This has been the theme of Indian philosophical pursuit since antiquity. As the *Brihadaranyaka Upanishad* notes:

> Verily, the Self is to be seen, to be heard, to be perceived, to be marked, Oh Maitreyi! When the Self has been seen, heard, perceived, and known, then all this is known.
>
> – IV.v.6 (Max Müller 1884/1995, *The Upanishads*, part II, Oxford: Clarendon Press, p.183)

Self-discovery is thus the goal; and *yoga* is a means to reach that goal.

Human mind is a mix of thinking, feeling, and action. In the existential situation we hardly find a stable balance between them. In one person, knowing may be a characteristic way of functioning. In another, it may be feeling or doing. Among most of us it is a mix of them. It is for this reason, the human mind is in a state of flux; and the need to control the ever-wandering states of the mind. Consequently, *yoga* needs to address the three types of people driven predominantly by thinking, feeling, or action. This calls for three basic kinds of *yoga* – *jnana* (knowledge), *bhakti* (devotion), and *karma* (action). Self-realization may be sought by pursuing the path of knowledge (*jnana-yoga*), devotion/faith (*bhakti-yoga*), or action (*karma-yoga*). However, the three are not exclusive.

One may combine them in various proportions. This happens often in most people, even though one characteristic element may be more dominant than others.

Now, we may not lose site of the fact that the self and the ego (the sense of I-ness) are not the same. Ego often masquerades as the self and acts as an obstruction to self-realization. Self-realization is not possible unless the ego is brought under control and eventually eliminated altogether. This calls for cultivating altruism as a pervasive value. Altruism involves overcoming the limitations of the self confined to a single identity, and extending it to include others, seeing the same/similar self in others as well.

Everyone, whether intellectually sophisticated or an illiterate person, seeks to know what lies beyond the present and to bridge the gap between the seen and the unseen. It is a necessary exercise for survival. So, philosophy becomes a part of one's existence. It gets articulated in philosophical writings as a quest for truth.

Again, what is apparent around is the vast sea of suffering. So the task is to swim to the shore and to avoid drowning in it. The quest for truth and overcoming suffering then become necessary and integral aspects of living. Knowing and doing get intertwined in the process. Knowing truth and deriving happiness from realizing it in one's being is the existential quest, an integral part of human endeavor.

Indian philosophy from antiquity to the present is, in a significant sense, pursuit of *yoga* to achieve a synthesis between the past, present, and future. *Yoga* is an endeavor to yoke the present with the past and the future. *Yoga* is thus an indispensable part of our lives. This is a basic assumption underlying Indian thought. The nature of yoking and implications from different perspectives is the main theme of Indian philosophical thought. Therefore, we may keep in mind that we have the responsibility, while living in the present, to remember the past and focus on the future. We should function as a bridge and live a wholesome life realizing the true self by serving others. Service above self should be the motive. Mahatma Gandhi, and his message, have eternal relevance inspiration and guiding our thought, passion and action.

There are three fundamental principles and eleven basic values underlying Gandhi's thought. The principles are:

(a) *sarvodaya*, which signifies that the good of the individual is what is good for all;

(b) dignity of labor, no work conscientiously done is inferior to any other; and

(c) reducing oneself to a zero, which means controlling and eventually eliminating the ego.

The eleven values that Gandhi endeavor to encourage in his followers are adherence to the principles of

1. nonviolence,
2. truth,
3. non-stealing,
4. celibacy,
5. non-possession,
6. bread-labor,
7. control of greed,
8. fearlessness and courage in the face of challenges,
9. respect for all faiths,
10. development of the spirit of *swadeshi*, which promotes self-respect, and
11. non-discrimination, and fighting against such practices as untouchability.

Gandhi became the Mahatma not for he acquired but what he gave. He possessed nothing and gave everything he has to his country, nay, to humanity.

Since the Narendra Modi government announced its smart city initiative in 2014, "smart" became a buzzword. There is talk of smart village, smart ward, smart card, smart phone, smart this, and smart that. Many of these usages ignore the real emphasis behind smart as in the concept "smart city" as it came to be developed in the West.

Dictionary definition of "smart" has various connotations. They range from "clean," "bright," "stylish," and "attractive" to "giving a sharp, stinging pain" and "feel upset and annoyed." Thus, smart may be used in a positive and optimistic sense or in a negative and derogatory way. Granting that the current use is clearly in the positive sense, we may not ignore the possibility of negative fallout. For example, many big cities in the West pride themselves of becoming smart cities by embracing information technology in the pursuit to improve city governance and conveniences. There is shift in emphasis from the outward concrete, glass, and steel structures to underground computers and software. Smart cities are now the growing places

> where information technology is wielded to address problems old and new. In the past, buildings and infrastructure shunted the flow of people and goods in rigid and predetermined ways. But smart cities can adapt on the fly, by pulling readings from vast arrays of sensors, feeding that data into software that can see the big picture, and consequently taking necessary action. They optimize cooling in buildings, balance the flow of electricity through the power grid, and keep transporting networks moving.
>
> – Townsend 2014, *Smart Cities: Big Data, Civic Hackers, and the Quest for a New Utopia*, p. 13
>
> New York: W.W. Norton

It is the case that application of technologies of information to governance and the organization of community activities is as old as human civilization. Development of languages, writing, printing, telegraph, telephone, radio, television, and now the smart phone are different variants of information technology. They have in many ways changed our lives. Then, they also bring with them new problems.

Smart city is no exception. First, as noticed during the past few years, tools available to new technology may foster unrest and citizen revolt as witnessed in the 2011 urban uprising of the Arab Spring. Such events may lead to blacking out of the wireless networks of the cities as it happened during the Egyptian uprising. Second, there is every likelihood that smart cities may worsen the gaps between haves and have-nots. Third, application of smart technologies may have unintended adverse consequences. Townsend writes:

> Even if there is peace and equality, the smart city may come crashing down under its own weight because it is already buggy, brittle, and bugged, and will only become more so.
>
> – Townsend, 2014, ibid.: 13

Finally, the new technologies provide enormous opportunities for governments and corporations to spy on citizens, employees, and consumers. This risk may not be taken lightly. The unintended adverse consequences of new technologies in the past sometimes outpaced their intended beneficial effects. Referring to the experience in the Western countries, Townsend points out:

> Motorization promised to save the city dwellers from the piles of horse manure that clogged nineteenth-century streets and deliver us from a shroud of factory smoke back to nature. Instead, it scarred the countryside with sprawl and rendered us sedentary and obese.
>
> – Townsend, 2014, ibid.: 14

As Visakhapatnam braces itself to become a smart city it serves us well to keep in mind the positive and negative sides of being smart.

Now, it seems to me, "smart" really refers to the mind of an individual or an organization. Like in the case of a human being who has body, mind, and spirit (soul), every organization may be seen as having body, mind, and spirit behind it. It is the spirit that guides the mind which in turn drives the body. Information technology with computers, software, and internet connectivity may be seen as the nervous system and the base of an organization's mind. The infrastructure and other physical facilities constitute its body.

Let us consider for a moment, the notion of a smart university. Smart university may be conceived as the one that makes maximum use of technology in its teaching and research. However, teaching and research useful to humankind cannot be carried out in a moral vacuum. In fact, an undisciplined and amoral mind with its smartness may do more harm than good. For the good of us, technology and values should go together. Without values guiding, technology is like a gun in the hands of a blind man.

It follows that universities need to be more than smart in their teaching and research. They need to employ not only the latest technologies but also embrace a wholesome value system to guide its activities. They should become super. I borrow the concept "super" from Sri Aurobindo.

What is a super university? How we may reach

that goal? I draw inspiration here from Gurudeva Rabindranath Tagore, Mahatma Gandhi, and Sri Aurobindo. The three are the *trimurti*s that stand out prominently as we turn the pages of twentieth-century intellectual history of India. In the confluence of their thought we find a genuine expression of Indian tradition at its best. The three are three *yogin*s, each in his own way. Gandhi's was the *yoga* of nonviolence. Sri Aurobindo articulated his integral *yoga*. Tagore was fully immersed in his literary *yoga*. *Yoga* is the pursuit toward perfection; and perfection consists in realizing and expressing truth in one's being.

Tagore famously said that the objective of education and universities for that matter is discovery and dissemination of truth. Gandhi repeatedly asserted that Truth is God; and that truth may be realized by selfless service. Gandhi called it *anasakti-yoga*. Sri Aurobindo provided a conceptual and philosophical framework of realizing truth in his formulation of psychic evolution. He calls such an evolution "Nature's method of self-transcendence" (Aurobindo 1970-75, *The Life Divine*: *Book Two Part Two*, Pondicherry: Sri Aurobindo Ashram, p. 737). "The first indispensable step in an upward evolution," he tells us, "would be to elevate our force of consciousness into those higher parts of Mind from which we already receive, but without knowing the source, much of our larger mental movements, those, especially, that come with a greater power and light, the revelatory, the inspirational, the intuitive" (ibid.: 736). Force of consciousness is none other than the moral force, what Gandhi called "truth-force" or "soul-force."

Sri Aurobindo suggests that psychic evolution involves a series of identifiable steps. He conceptualizes them as (1) Higher Mind, (2) Illumined Mind, (3) Intuitive Mind, (4) Overmind, and (5) Supermind. These successive "self-transmutations," as he calls them, "are domains of being, grades of the substance and energy of the spiritual being. ..." (ibid.: 938). This is the evolution of the Higher Mind or psychic evolution, which makes the mind more receptive to reflect with less distortion and greater perfection the light of consciousness by controlling its own lower functions.

Now, the task of super university of my conception is to help plant in students the seeds of Supermind. The Supermind is the true spirit of education. It is education with values. It is education for self-transformation. It is the wholesome confluence of the three – body, mind, and spirit – that makes teaching and learning a truly transformative experience.

It is not unreasonable to do so because we earned that right in virtue of our age and past experience. However, I deviate from such a practice because I am aware as a psychologist that advices that are not consistent with the recipient's behavioral disposition often go unheeded. If it is consistent, then, there would be no need for giving it. A better strategy in my view is to provide an analysis rather than advice, using one's own expertise and experience.

It is natural to tell the students to keep their growing minds calm and free from conflicts, cultivate conflict-free conduct, and consequently enjoy peace and tranquility. It would be a good advice coming from an old man like me because what I need at this stage of my life is peace of mind. I am afraid, however, it is not so for the growing minds. In fact, no mind can be free from conflicts. It is in the nature of the mind and how it works. Indeed there can be no progress without conflict. Life is a field of choices. Successful people are those who make right choices.

Progress is a dialectical process, where there is a contest between what is and what could be, which is resolved by creatively carving a synthesis of the opposing claims. Human development itself is a dialectical process. As Mahatma Gandhi has repeatedly brought to our attention, the person is a composite of devil and divine, the beast and the man, as he termed them. The goal of human pursuit is to overcome the devil and experience the divine within. The conflict situation is always a contest between alternatives. The task is to choose the one closer to truth. Truth is an ideal which one never reaches, but something he strives for. Therefore, compromise is necessarily built into proper truth-seeking exercise.

Compromise is not bending truth, but coming closer to it. It consists in a meaningful synthesis of competing alternatives. It involves a win-win situation. There are no losers or winners. Everyone benefits by getting closer to truth.

The young people with inquisitive minds are about to enter a stage in their lives where conflicts will be routine rather than exceptional, whether it is interpersonal between husband and wife or professional among coworkers. It would be a myth to think that there would be no conflicts if you cultivate proper behavior and attitudes. I know of no wife and husband who did not experience conflict in their relationship at some point in their lives. One cannot escape conflicts by avoiding them. They are bound to occur. The beauty of life is how one deals with them. Conflicts seen as competing claims of truth and attempting to reach a compromise by finding a meaningful synthesis is the best way of getting closer to truth. It would be an opportunity to convert challenges into opportunities; an occasion to grow mentally and morally.

Mahatma Gandhi's life is an excellent case of an inspiring person who made right choices and converted challenges into opportunities.

9

Unexpected Assignments

To continue the story of my tryst with destiny, I was in Delhi to attend a national seminar on Indian psychology at University of Delhi. At that time, Shri Kavuri Sambasiva Rao popularly known as K.S. Rao was a Member of Parliament. He is related to Dr. M.V.V.S. Murthi, whom I have known for a long time. I paid a courtesy call on K.S. Rao. He enquired about what I was doing; and then asked me to go with him to meet the Joint Secretary of Education Shri Sunil Kumar in his office. He was obviously interested in exploring if my services could be used in Delhi. He never mentioned this to me. It so happened that the Joint Secretary had on his desk the file relating to the appointment of chairman of the Indian Council of Philosophical Research (ICPR) to be forwarded to the prime minister for his approval. Apparently, he was not quite satisfied with the credentials of the person being recommended by the then HRD Minister Shri Arjun Singh. On learning about my background, the Joint Secretary asked me if he could have a written note about my academic background. It was hardly possible for me to prepare a vitae in such a hurry. Fortunately, it so happened that I had with me a copy of the book edited by Dr. K.S. Chalam as a *Festschrift* on my 70th birthday. The book contained a complete bibliography of my writings upto 2002. We hurriedly got a xerox copy of the bibliography and passed it on to the Joint Secretary. The secretary attached my brief CV and the bibliography to the file along with that of the person recommended by the HRD minister and forwarded them to the prime minister. Dr. Manmohan Singh was the prime minister then. He chose my name to be the next chairman of the ICPR in place of Dr. Kireet Joshi, just retired. I did not seek that position. Nor was I expecting it. Again, the hand of destiny!

This unexpected assignment turned out eventful in more than one way. First, it gave me national exposure. Until then my interactions in India were limited to Andhra University and in a small way extended to Andhra Pradesh. Second, my work until then was focused more on psychology than on philosophy. Now a significant shift in the area of my academic involvement. Third, I was able to reconnect with my roots. It was an occasion to realize the goal I had in mind when I started my academic journey prompted by my early mentor, Prof. Saileswar Sen. Finally, I hate to say this, the ICPR itself was in a bad shape; and in some ways it was in a dysfunctional state. The Chairman, Shri Kireet Joshi, a bachelor without family, was literally living in Darshan Bhavan that houses the ICPR. So it was a special challenge to resurrect and revive ICPR, and make it play its due national and international roles as envisaged in its charter and help to promote studies of Indian philosophy in India and around the world.

My appointment as Chairman of ICPR was for a period of three years, which was later got extended for another term of three years. To begin with, I had to choose my priorities:

- The first concern was to reorganize the office.
- The second item on the agenda was to find the necessary resources.
- The third concern was to take the ICPR away from its isolation and lead it to work in liaison with other national organizations such as the Indian Council of Social Science Research, and give it an interdisciplinary perspective.
- Fourth, there was a strong need to establish regional centers. Philosophy manifests in various shades and stripes in different parts of the country, each with its own unique identity, culture, and tradition. There is thus the need to recognize and protect these different identities.
- Fifth, I strongly felt that Indian philosophy needs a worldwide platform and should make its presence felt internationally.
- Sixth, there should be more effective communication among Indian scholars involved in philosophy, who appeared to be somewhat isolated, functioning with little communication with fellow scholars. The annual conferences of Indian Philosophy Congress were insufficient to build necessary channels of communication.
- Seventh, the ICPR had a national library

originally located at Butler Palace in Lucknow, which was designated as enemy property since the Muslim owner of the Palace fled to Pakistan. Consequently, in my opinion unwisely, the ICPR hurriedly vacated the palace premises, and stored the books in a close-by public library. There was hardly any reading room place. Earlier the Palace had rooms for scholars coming from outside of Lucknow to stay and make use of the library. So, the national asset of a good philosophy library fell into near disuse.

- Finally, philosophy needs to be presented as a relevant discipline for actual living. Therefore, its applied aspects require emphasis along with its historic aspects guiding human conduct and social responsibilities and interaction.

In some ways, I was a stranger in Delhi. I needed to develop appropriate contacts with higher-ups in the government so that I could pursue my ambitious agenda. I successfully tried and gained access to the HRD Minister, Shri Arjun Singh. I initiated at the ICPR, the Life Time Achievement Award in Philosophy. We chose Prof. K. Satchidananda Murty as the first recipient of the award. By then Prof. Murty took to *vanaprastha* and had no interest in worldly rewards. So, as Chairman of the ICPR, I personally went to his house in his village Sangam Jagarlamudi and handed over the award to his children.

The next recipients of the award were D.P. Chattopadhyaya and Prof. R. Balasubramanian. I invited the prime minister to present the awards. Dr. Manmohan Singh graciously agreed; and now I got to know personally the prime minister. My stock as the Chairman of ICPR went up. I was ready to play a major role in reshaping and breathing new life into ICPR.

The priority item was to relocate the ICPR Library in Lucknow. We had in the library more than 30,000 volumes and subscribed to over 100 philosophy journals and received many more on exchange. All these needed to be properly stacked and displayed. I looked around and found that the UP government had just built a nice building for a public library, which was still unoccupied. I met the chief minister of UP Ms. Mayavati and successfully negotiated with the concerned officials to move the ICPR Library into this new building. It was a huge relief; and for me, it was the taste of a first major success.

The next move was to take steps to highlight Indian philosophy in world philosophy forums. Towards this end, I led delegations of Indian philosophers to participate in the forums of World Congress of Philosophy (WCP). This took us first to St. Petersburg in Russia and then to Seoul in South Korea, where we made our presence felt. ICPR had arranged for example a roundtable discussion at WCP in Seoul. Fred Dallmayr, George McLean among others participated in it.

Another major step in the internationalization of Indian philosophy was the organization of the First

Asian Philosophy Congress during 6-9 March 2010 at Jawaharlal Nehru University in New Delhi.

It is indeed very satisfying to look back and note several programs that we initiated and carried out at the ICPR during the my period as the Chairman (2006-12). We organized annually ICPR Fellows meet, presented awards to deserving scholars, and got to know first hand the progress of the work being carried out by young scholars. We invited distinguished persons like Dr. Karan Singh to address and inspire the new generation of scholars pursuing philosophical studies. ICPR helped to organize periodical lectures to popularize philosophy at various institutions across the country involving senior scholars hailing from that area. We invited eminent Indian philosophers and scholars from abroad specializing in Indian thought and arranged for their lectures at various institutions in the country. We helped to organize refresher courses in philosophy on different philosophical themes for college and university teachers. The ICPR also provided travel grants to Indian scholars to participate in international events. Further, we had attempted to encourage interdisciplinary studies, and sought to emphasize applied aspects of philosophy. Also, ICPR sought to promote international collaboration and academic linkages with other countries. We organized annually International Philosophy Day on a large scale. I myself travelled to other countries such as Iran in 2010 and participated in the International Philosophy Day. We may recall that the UNESCO declared the third Thursday in November as

International Philosophy Day to commemorate the birth anniversary of Socrates.

We instituted several awards to promote philosophical studies and research in the country and to recognize outstanding achievements. These included in addition to the

1. Life Time Achievement Award mentioned earlier,

2. Best Dissertation Award,

3. Best Book of the Year in Philosophy Award, and

4. Young Philosophers Award.

I may mention two additional events that are still fresh in my mind. We organized two seminars on national integration – one at the Indian Institute of Advanced Studies in Simla, and the other at the North-Eastern Hill University in Shillong. The participants included such luminaries as Dr. Abid Hussain and Shri Sitaram Yechuri. Dr. Asghar Ali Engineer, Balachander Mungekar (at the time Member of Planning Commission), and Shri Y.B. Yugandhar (another Member of Planning Commission) were among the other participants who brought with them diverse perspectives, from economic, social, religious, philosophical, and political fields. One has to go through the issues of *ICPR Newsletter* to learn more about the breadth of ICPR activities at the time. The *Newsletter* served as an important tool to facilitate communication among students and scholars of philosophy in the country. It is a pity that the *Newsletter* ceased publication soon after my leaving the ICPR. Indeed it was painful that the last issue of the *Newsletter* that was set in print and was ready to be released was abruptly withdrawn by my successor.

The second event I look back with some pride is the organization of Gandhirama at Jawaharlal Nehru University in New Delhi. It was an international event attended by several foreign participants and a large number of Indian scholars coming from different disciplines. We have specially invited Saths Cooper as a distinguished speaker. Dr. Cooper is an Indian descendant from South Africa. He was a fellow prisoner along with Nelson Mandela, and rose to become the President of International Psychology Congress. By any standards, the first edition of Gandhirama was a huge success. Its success warranted a second edition which was held at GITAM University in Visakhapatnam. It was again a large gathering of Gandhian scholars. We also had interesting exhibits of *khadi* and weavers working on making *khadi*. It is time now to think of the grand finale, the third edition of Gandhirama, to coincide with Mahatma's 150th birth anniversary in 2019.

More personally satisfying than the activities mentioned above, indeed are my own scholarly research contributions during this period. I published the voluminous *Cognitive Anomalies, Consciousness and Yoga*, which brings together and integrates the three main areas of my intellectual pursuit for over one half of a century. This book was widely reviewed and well received.

David Lorimer, Program Director of the Scientific and Medical Network based in Paris, has the following to say:

> Ramakrishna Rao's prodigious output over the last ten years has amounted to over 5,000 pages, including the magisterial *Cognitive Anomalies, Consciousness and Yoga*, which I reviewed for the *Journal of Consciousness Studies*. He is an interdisciplinary giant who has integrated his ideas across many disciplines, while never losing sight of the fundamental importance of wisdom, the process of spiritualization, and applied spirituality addressed to the fundamental challenges of our time.

During this period I also published *Gandhi and Applied Spirituality* (2011). I attempted in this volume to go beyond the pragmatic aspect of Gandhi's thought and actions first in South Africa and later in India, and to emphasize in addition the spiritual foundations of Mahatma's philosophy and practices and their contemporary relevance for a world in turmoil. In the current global scenario and the availability of weapons of mass destruction even to small countries like North Korea, violence is no longer a viable option for conflict resolution. Violence has become irrelevant and even self-destructive for those adopting it. Elsewhere, I elaborated on the thesis that *satyagraha* as an instrument of conflict resolution has spiritual roots. Uprooted from its spiritual foundation, *satyagraha* as an instrument of social action loses its very essence as practiced by Gandhi.

Invitation from GITAM University

As I was completing my second term as the chairman of the ICPR, GITAM University invited me to be its Chancellor. I was already 80 years old, and reluctant to assume any new responsibilities. That was the reason why I did not seek any other assignments in Delhi. I had close links with several people in power; it would have been a simple matter to find another important national assignment in the Indian government. However, I accepted the invitation from GITAM for two main reasons. First, Chancellor is a ceremonial figure who presides over the annual convocations with no other administrative responsibilities. Second, GITAM is located in Visakhapatnam, which is now the place of my residence.

With the mind still active, it was difficult to spend time in retirement. GITAM at the time was entirely an engineering institution. It needed to build a base in humanities and social sciences. Further, GITAM was named after Gandhi. Under the leadership of Dr. M.V.V.S. Murthi, it was making major strides on many fronts. Dr. Murthi was keen to promote Gandhian studies. It was difficult to resist the temptation of building a school of Gandhian Studies and begin a new chapter in my own life. So I am here at 86 chairing the School of Gandhian Studies at GITAM and looking after its humanities and social sciences wings.

Living up to my expectations, GITAM built a huge new building appropriately named as Sarvodaya Soudha for housing the School of Gandhian Studies, provided provision for recruiting necessary faculty, and encouraged me in every possible way with the aim of making the School a truly internationally acknowledged Center for Gandhian Studies and Research. We have a long way to go; but the goal is set, and the path is now clearly marked. We have already associated with it several internationally acknowledged scholars and experts, who include the renowned writer and psychoanalyst Dr. Sudhir Kakar, Prof. Rama Rao Pappu, Emeritus Professor from USA, Sushil Mittal from George Mason University in USA, Dr. Anand Paranjpe, Emeritus Professor from Simon Fraser University in Canada, and Dr. Savita Singh, former Director of Gandhi Smriti and Darsan Samiti in New Delhi. We also have to advise us some of the distinguished former administrative leaders such as Shri Padmanabiah, who served as Home Secretary in Government of India. The above are among the visiting faculty who supplement the regular resident faculty.

Another important addition is the starting of a three-year integrated undergraduate program in social sciences. The uniqueness of this program is that all the social science courses are taught against the backdrop of Gandhian thought and practices with the goal of training future leaders in public, private, and political sectors, who place service above self in a Gandhian mode.

In addition to teaching and training young minds, we are engaged at GITAM in some in-depth research activities. Since pursuit of nonviolence involves as a first step avoidance of violence, we attempted to study the nature and varieties of violence. Along with Prof. Sambasiva Prasad I brought together a large collection of papers under the title *Phenomenology of Violence* (2018). Dr. Nalini Bikkina (2014, "Gandhian Perspective of Violence and Alternatives to Violence", *GITAM Journal of Gandhian Studies*, 3(1): 150-207) published an extensive paper on Gandhian conception of violence and his alternatives to it. Recognizing that violence consists not only in hurting other human beings but also in degrading the environment, the Mahatma pleaded for ecological nonviolence as well. So, environmental activism has become a subject of study by GITAM's staff. Dr. A.S. Sasikala (2014, "Gandhi and Environmental Activism: A Study of Indian Environmental Movements", *GITAM Journal of Gandhian Studies,* 3(2): 465-80) has already published on this topic; and the work continues.

GITAM with its extensive agenda for Gandhian studies needed its own vehicle of communication. So we started the *GITAM Journal of Gandhian Studies*, which has already six volumes to its credit. A special feature of the journal is that half of its pages are devoted for publishing Gandhi's original writings.

My involvement with GITAM's School of Gandhian Studies is more than lending my name to it. I am actively engaged in research and writings. One of the fruits is *Gandhi's Dharma* (2017a) published by Oxford University Press, as mentioned earlier. My interest in Gandhi's *yoga* of nonviolence led me to the study and research on *yoga* and meditation. An outcome of this interest is the book *Foundations of Yoga Psychology* (2017b). In the place of Gandhi's concept of *swadeshi*, we increasingly find the *videshi* mindset in modern India, a consequence of two centuries of British colonial rule, which I call the colonial syndrome. Colonial syndrome is another subject of my current interest. The book *Colonial Syndrome: The Videshi Mindset in Modern India* has come out recently (2018); and Hon'ble Shri Venkaiah Naidu, Vice-President of India, formally released it on 24 August 2018. I have the satisfaction of dedicating this book to him because he is a true *swadeshi* and an illustrious antithesis of the colonial syndrome.

As mentioned, my interest in Gandhi and his relevance to the today's troubled world leads me beyond studying Gandhi to promote Gandhian ideas and practices around the world. Now, therefore, my focus is to help craft instruments, pave the path, find the vehicles to move forward, and spread Gandhi's life and message of nonviolence across the globe in a tangible manner, at least to make a small beginning toward achieving it in this part of the world. The *mantra* of *ahimsa* as chanted by the Mahatma appears to be the only means of saving humankind from self-destruction.

Ahimsa: The Mantra to Save Humankind from Self-Destruction

According to legend, we are in Kaliyuga, possibly at its terminal point. Now, whether it would end with a terrible bang (*pralaya*) or whether we could make a smooth transition to the new age should be a matter of considerable interest to futurologists. If competition is necessary and violence is the way to fight for survival, it is reasonable to expect a *pralaya*. However, if we could adopt nonviolence as a means of change, there is a hope for a non-turbulent turnaround. Mahatma Gandhi strongly believed that a tranquil transition is possible if nonviolence becomes the guiding value. He had experimented throughout his mature life, how nonviolence (*ahimsa*) could be practiced in different facets of living, including as a means of conflict resolution.

Gandhi believed that humans are a composite of animal and spiritual. The animal drives them toward violence. If appropriately cultivated the spiritual helps to manifest the divine within. The proper means of cultivating the spiritual is the practice of *ahimsa* (nonviolence). Nonviolence in life should manifest in one's thought, passion, and action, in what one believes, says, and does.

Ahimsa is more than not killing others; it is beyond refraining from destroying the environment and depleting natural resources. In its positive sense, nonviolence involves love, loving others, and the surroundings. Gandhi said repeatedly, where there is love, there is life. The path of the truth, according to Mahatma, is the path of nonviolence.

Loving others as much as you love yourself is genuine love. It is limitless and unbounded. It does not discriminate. Love is spiritual; it is uplifting. It is contagious and irresistible. It radiates like the sun; and calms one like the moon. It is a positive force. Saying is one thing; and doing is another. Harmonious blend of the two is what is called for. Mahatma asserted repeatedly two things. First, believe in what you say; and do what you say. Second, be the change that you want to see.

Violence outlived its utility as a means of conflict resolution. Even small countries have the technologies and resources to cause widespread destruction around the world. Therefore, *ahimsa* is the only instrument that can prevent mass destruction, which includes self-destruction.

It is in our tradition to chant *om shanti, shanti, shantih* (Peace Unto All), at the conclusion of all ceremonies. We have much to learn from this practice. *Ahimsa* is the means to reach the state of peace, preservation of the person, and the realization of the self.

Chanting of the *mantra* of *ahimsa* is the way to reach the pinnacle of perpetual peace. It is the most appropriate resource that would help, guide, and lead us to reach the true source of love. When we reach there, we find ourselves at the fountain of joy; and climb the peak of the mountain from where we can have a pervasive look at the panorama of life with all its wonders and many-sided splendors.

As mentioned, *ahimsa* is a positive force. It is not living a reclusive life. It is involved in selfless service to others in need. The Mahatma was never tired of saying: "Hands that help are holier than lips that pray."

Service is at the root of *ahimsa*. In rendering service, one should reduce himself/herself to nothing, which means that there should be no ego involvement. It is selfless; service qua service. It is service for the sake of service. Only such service that transcends the ego is genuine. Service with self at the center is spurious. It is pseudo service that masquerades in false and pretentious robes. It is malicious and misleading.

The Mahatma had proclaimed that his life was his message. What does this mean? It means that his thought was conveyed by his actions. His life was a harmonious blend of thought, passion, and action. It indeed is the signal characteristic of the Mahatma, the great soul that continues to inspire humankind. Gandhi did not receive the Nobel Award. However, several that traveled on the path he laid did. What could be a greater tribute!

To get back to the theme of *ahimsa*, I would like to repeat and re-emphasize that there is no alternative to the ethics of nonviolence to save humankind from self destruction. As parents, we should instill the value of nonviolence in our children. As teachers, we should drill into the minds of our students, the *mantra* of *ahimsa*. It should be a ritual, as a daily exercise. Those in public life should display nonviolence in their conduct. These are some of the ways to propagate nonviolence as a way of life.

Understanding the nature and forms of its manifestation is necessary for dealing effectively with violence.

Varieties of Violence

Violence is the real threat for continuing survival of our species. In order to control and eradicate it we need to understand the variety of forms violence takes and its varied manifestations in our lives.

There are many kinds of violence. It originates in many ways, manifests in different forms, and comes in various shades and different intensities. It is necessary to understand the varieties of violence and how they arise so that we may gain a measure of control over it.

In a significant sense, violence is in man's nature. Mahatma Gandhi repeatedly asserted that man is a composite of the animal and the divine. The animal in him instinctively drives man to violent ways of reaching the goals, whereas the divine in him is the spiritual force that helps to generate love and achieve a state of self-realization. Man's ultimate goal is self-realization. Consequently the main step toward reaching this goal is cultivation of love.

Love may be self-centered or other-directed. The former is tied to the ego and is prompted by the animal side of human nature, which is self-preservation and survival. The latter is driven by the divine within; it is altruistic. The best and sure way of achieving self-realization, as the Mahatma has repeatedly mentioned, is to find the true self, which, according to him is to lose oneself in the service of others. This would be possible when one reduces himself to a zero or nothing, i.e. total elimination of involvement of the ego in action.

Violence is turbulent, disturbing, and destructive whereas love is placid, tranquilizing, and conducive to creative generation. Violence is instinctive to man's animal origins; but love is something to be cultivated. Therefore, significant effort is required to control violent tendencies and to plant the seeds of love in the mind.

Violence may be in thought, feeling, or action. Thinking of harm to others is violence in thought. Enjoying the suffering of others is violence in feeling. Actually doing things to hurt others is violence in action.

Violence may be physical or psychological. Physical violence is hurting others by inflicting external injury such as stabbing someone. Psychological violence may be seen in insulting and hurting the feelings of others. Violence may be against a person or a group of persons. Or it may be against environment and nature.

Exploitation of others to serve one's selfish goals is a common form of violence. Violence may be against children as in child abuse. Violence may be against elderly by neglect, failure to pay due respect, and even coercing them to act against their wishes. It may be against one's own self as in suicide. Any kind of exploitation, whether economic, social, or sexual is violence. Political vendetta is another form of violence. Any kind of discrimination such as racial, religious, or regional is a form of violence.

Why do people engage in violence? First, as mentioned, it is instinctive, prompted by the animal nature in humans. Violence is sometimes simple imitative behavior. It may be a gameplay.

Violence can be perpetuated by a person or group of persons, as in communal violence. It may be between states as in wars.

Media play a significant role in planting seeds of violence in peoples' mind. As often mentioned, wars originate in the minds of men. By highlighting violence for good or bad, press keeps the notion of violence alive and active in the minds of people. Instead, stories of violence need to be sidelined and reported marginally, while the episodes of love and nonviolence should be prominently presented. Presently the reverse is the case. We have museums with war memorials such as airplanes, submarines, and so on. In fact, the beautiful beach adjoining Ramakrishna Mission in Visakhapatnam is literally littered with reminders of violence and war. What we need to display prominently instead are the icons of peace. Surprisingly, while we have statues of many heroes at Ramakrishna beach, the statue of Mahatma Gandhi is conspicuous by its absence.

Bengaluru is a beautiful city. It is blessed by nature with comfortable weather conditions. It is our responsibility, rather duty, to preserve the pristine natural beauty and prevent it from all kinds of pollution. Again, pollution may be in thought, word, or action. All the three kinds of pollution should be effectively dealt with in an unsparing manner.

10

Concluding Thoughts

IN THIS CONCLUDING CHAPTER, I wish to reflect on some of the salient aspects of my professional activities and academic studies. In the first place, why did I get involved in parapsychology, which consumed a major part of my professional career? The simple answer is that I see the hand of destiny more than any inherent desire to become a parapsychologist. It is true that I have had a consuming interest in understanding human nature. Psychology was, therefore, a subject of significant interest. So, I chose it as an elective in my BA (Hons) course at Andhra University. However, it would be misleading to suggest or imply that I was naturally led to study and specialize in it. In fact, I joined the BA (Hons) philosophy program at Andhra University after failing to secure admission in what seemed at that time more lucrative subjects of study. My first choice would have been medicine. The next was science. When those options were foreclosed, destiny drove me to join the philosophy program at Andhra University. However, after joining, when I had an option to choose, I elected to study psychology.

Psychology at Andhra University at that time was taught along with philosophy. What we were learning in our philosophy classes (especially Indian philosophy) was in sharp contrast with what we were being taught in psychology courses. The concept of *Brahman* that Professor Sen was so passionately explained seemed utterly irreconcilable with what we were taught in our psychology courses with a behaviorist slant. So, I confronted Prof. Sen in one of his classes and raised questions about the scientific validity of the notion of *Brahman*. I asked pointedly how we may reconcile the two, since they seem to be mutually exclusive. With a broad smile on his face, Prof. Sen asked me to meet him after the class in his office. When I met him, Prof. Sen told me that there is a way to reconcile. He asked me to read F.W.H. Myers two volume *Human Personality and Its Survival of Death* (1915, London: Longmans Green and Co.), and J.B. Rhine's monograph *Extra-Sensory Perception* (1935, Boston: Humphries.). These books were available in Andhra University Library. After reading them, I chose to do my MA (Hons) dissertation on the subject of paranormal cognition, describing Eastern and Western approaches for studying it. This resulted in the publication of the book *Psi Cognition* (1957), more than sixty years ago. At my request, J.B. Rhine contributed the Foreword; and I became acquainted with him. This was the beginning of the long professional journey in that field. From that very humble beginning, I managed to climb to a point that I headed Rhine's own establishment for nearly two decades.

Why did I move away from parapsychology in more recent years? The drift is quite natural, because my cultural roots are elsewhere. My involvement in parapsychology was to find a bridge between Eastern thought and Western science, between the spiritual experience and scientific search for self-realization. When pursuit of parapsychological research became an end in itself, I was caught in a sort of vicious circle. The main purpose of my getting involved in it got defeated. It took me over two decades to discover that my work in parapsychology was an artificial transplant in the alien soil of Western science, while my natural roots were in Indian spirituality. This has led me in recent years to a more in-depth study of psychology contained in classical Indian tradition, *yoga* in particular.

Yoga seems to be the discipline that bridges the gap between science and spirituality. This had naturally taken me among other things to study Patanjali's *Yogasutra* in some detail. One of the fruits of this endeavor is my recent book, *Patanjali's Yogasutra: A Psychological Study* (2018). Working on this book was a truly satisfying exercise; and I am indeed glad that I undertook this task.

Now, my engagement with *yoga* has further aroused my curiosity to delve more into my native thought. This has led me to undertake a study of *Bhagavadgita* from a psychological perspective. The result is my book *Bhagavadgita: A Psychological Journey* (2019).

My interest in Mahatma Gandhi dates back to my student days. I grew up when the country was fighting for freedom from colonial rule; and the Mahatma was leading it. I was a student leader who was inspired by Gandhi's message, from the Quit India Movement, the Noakhali incidents, and Gandhi's fast. The poignant memories of his assassination still haunt me. Now it is all too clear that violence outlived its utility as a tool of conflict resolution. *Ahimsa* appears to be the *mantra* to save the mankind from the peril of self-destruction. Writing the book *Gandhi's Dharma* (2017) gave me a number of new insights into the nuances of Gandhian thought and practices.

How did I get involved in Indian psychology? What is the rationale behind it? More specifically, what was it that led me to study *yoga* and get absorbed in it during recent years? Finally, about my interest in Mahatma Gandhi and why do I think that his ideas and practices are more globally relevant at the current period than during his own time? These questions were already addressed in the preceding pages.

My recent engagement is with developing the concept of "colonial syndrome," the *videshi* mindset, which is still pervasive among Indians after more than one half of a century since India became a republic. How may we overcome this severe drawback in our private and public lives despite our loud slogans of nationalism? Again, we find the relevance of Gandhi's concept of *swadeshi* to current affairs.

As we all know, life is more like a flowing stream rather than a still pond. There are natural ebbs and tides. What were the noticeable ups and downs in my own life? How did I endeavor to cope with turbulences during troubled times and control ecstasy while tasting success? What lessons have I learnt so that I might maintain equanimity? Equanimity is not keeping quiet, but striking a balance between positive and negative states of the mind, finding stability amidst changes.

I have occupied various positions at local as well as national levels. What is the role that gave me the greatest personal satisfaction? What were the situations that I found very frustrating and disturbing? I carried out studies and researches in a number of different areas. What is it that I value most? If I lead fifteen more years of active life, what will I do professionally? As I look back into my past, do I have any regrets? If I were to relive the past, would I do things any differently?

According to Gandhi, man's span of life is 125 years. Had it not been for the assassin's bullets, I believe, the Mahatma would have lived close to that goal of 125 years. Therefore, if I, inspired as I am by Gandhi, look ahead for fifteen more years, it may not be construed as an unrealistic expectation. What would I do, then, with the remainder of my life? Publish more books? Make more visits to USA? Spend quite time with family? Accumulate additional wealth?

In the Indian tradition, this period in one's life is the time to retire from active life, enter *vanaprastha ashrama*, and spend time in seclusion meditating on the meaning of life. In my own experience, I have the example of my teacher and friend Prof. K. Satchidananda Murty who was in that state of existence during the last few years of his life.

My mindset is, however, clearly alien to retirement. It is my wish to die leading an active rather than a reclusive life without being disabled in any serious way. So, tradition or no tradition, *vanaprastha* is ruled out. Also, making money and accumulating wealth is not an option. I have reached a stage in my life that I want to give rather than take any from others. The other options are not exclusive of each other. One can spend time with family and at the same time involve in social activities. One may write books and also travel, foster fresh friendships, and develop new interests. I would love to do all of them to the extent possible in the years ahead.

I am enjoying my work at GITAM; and I will continue to be actively associated with it. I spend now half day on GITAM campus. I work all afternoons in my office at home. The second floor of my house serves as my office. I have full-time secretarial services and other kinds of needed help available. Even though I have gifted the major part of my personal library of over 3,000 volumes to GITAM University, I still have in my office the needed reference and relevant volumes to consult. Thus, the necessary infrastructure is in place to continue my academic adventures from home office with no serious handicaps.

We have a submarine museum at a prominent location in Visakhapatnam on the beach, near the Ramakrishna Mission. Opposite to it, is an exhibit of a war plane. These are all meant to attract tourists. However, they do not add beauty to the seashore.

The war memorials may invoke in people the spirit of patriotism and sacrifice; but they equally remind us of violence and deaths. There are statues of several eminent persons. However, Gandhi's statue is conspicuous by its absence. May we not also have some structures and memorials to inspire nonviolence and invoke peace in the minds of visitors? It is my wish, hope, and prayer that we erect an iconic *shanti stupa*, an impressive pillar of peace visible to all the people in the city of Visakhapatnam.

The upcoming 150th birth anniversary of Mahatma Gandhi is an excellent opportunity to promote peace and take steps to help to develop the mindset of nonviolence in people. It is a perverted thought to think that only instruments of violence would attract tourists. There is nothing that leads people away from visiting the exhibits and structures designed to promote peace and nonviolence. We need to continually remind people that with all the destructive weapons on hand and terrorism riding high in the world, the spread of the ethic of nonviolence is a necessary antidote; and it provides the strategy required to ensure the survival of humankind.

My dream is to help build across the world what may be called Mahatma Gandhi Mandirs. By *mandir* we do not mean temple. I know at least one person who wants to build Gandhi temples. This in my view is contrary to the spirit of Mahatma. We mean by *mandir* a place to inspire. It is a place to create awareness on Gandhi's lifestyle, struggle for freedom, his ideology, and practices. It is a place where one finds inner peace.

It is a place to promote Gandhi's ideas (*shruti*), his *dharma* (*smriti*), and culture (*samskriti*). In my conception and visualization, the Mahatma Gandhi Mandir would include: (1) a museum, (2) research library and learning center, (3) a park, and (4) an open air theatre. The museum would contain:

a. Exhibits portraying Mahatma's life and practices, his insights into human nature, India of his dreams, and his initiatives to end exploitation and achieve social justice and equality.

b. Research library and learning center would have a well-stocked library and a bookstore containing Gandhian literature. It would have residential facilities for scholars coming from outside the city to use the library.

c. The park would be a place to inspire in people the spirit of *swadeshi*, to popularize handicrafts, and promote creative arts.

d. The open-air theatre would hold mass awareness programs on Mahatma Gandhi's life and the messege of peace and nonviolence throughout the year with periodic lectures by eminent scholars and practitioners of nonviolence in its multiple forms.

Mahatma is revered as the Father of the Nation. We mark his birth anniversary as a national day. We have his statues in many places. He thus remains an iconic figure. Beyond that, I regret to note, the new generations of Indians have little understanding of the life and practices of the Mahatma, which have so many lessons to offer for living a peaceful and happy life. I feel strongly that the life of Gandhi should be a subject taught to all students before they complete high-school education. The reading of Gandhi's *Autobiography: My Experiments with Truth* should be a must to all college-going students. The goal is to help the student develop an experimental habit of mind and not to accept anything without conviction. Our school education in my opinion still suffers from its colonial inheritance. We need to drastically revise the curriculum. We may not, however, rule out the use of the appropriate technology available. The basics of Gandhian education still hold good, even in the technological age. I would consider it a priority to help develop suitable methods of instruction following Gandhi's model of Nai Talim. They would be the necessary corrective to the mechanical and technocratic mindset in people; and it would be a wholesome addition to the human side in one's professional life.

Gandhi was not against the use of technology, as long as it does not control our lives, and becomes our master. Man needs to have full control over the instruments he uses and not otherwise. Just as globalization has come to stay, technology has invaded nearly every aspect of human functioning. It does seem to be an irreversible fact. What we need to do then is to promote checks and balances to prevent technology's adverse effects. Just as we need to develop rural culture in urban areas, we need to ensure that technology has its human side. This in my view calls for training our technocrats suitably, which in turn involves teaching humanities as a necessary and compulsory part of technological education. We need to redraw the curricular map of technological education providing appropriate places for humanities and social sciences.

Is there a need to write more books on Gandhi? Yes, I think, there is. There is need for popular and yet responsible rendering of Gandhian thought and practices, books suitable to create the mindset of truth, nonviolence, and altruism in the growing young minds. These narratives should include real-life stories, illustrative of the intrinsic value of truth and nonviolence. Also, we need to present along with it adequate information on the potential harm of violence with true life examples.

I am one of those who believe that we are not entirely what we want to be. In a significant sense, we are children of destiny. I mean by destiny the circumstances that drive our lives. Therefore, the question of reliving the past is not quite relevant. We may recall the past; but we will not be able to relive it, because we cannot recreate the past circumstances. In other words, the past cannot be reshaped; in life, we cannot take a step backward. However, we can shape our future and influence our destiny, keeping in mind the past and the lessons it holds for us. Man desires and destiny dispenses. It is something that I learnt in my eighty-five years of existence.

This, then, is a brief story of a child of destiny.

Photo Gallery

Professor K. Ramakrishna Rao

With beloved wife Smt K. Sarojini Devi

With his wife in 1960's

With his six grandchildren -
Vivek, Shilpa, Sunila, Kavya, Mira and Tarun

From Left, H. Kanthamani (student & colleague), Chandu (son),
Rani (daughter), Sarojini (wife), Shanti (student & colleague), Vani (daughter)

With his children and their spouses
Standing: Murali, Chandu, Rani and Sarat
Sitting: Mridula, Sarojini and Vani

Playing with his grandchild

Sri Zail Singh, President of India inaugurating the Institute of Yoga and Consciousness at Andhra University.
Dr. Shankar Dayal Sharma, Governor of Andhra Pradesh on the Dias.

Receiving *Padma Shri* award from Smt Pratibha Patil, President of India

Shri Kapil Sibal, Hon'ble Minister of Human Resource and Development, releasing the book *Cognitive, Anomalies, Consciousness and Yoga*. Professor Ramakrishna Rao's magnum opus

At California Institute for Human Science

Shri Abid Hussain, former Member of Planning Commission and Dr. M.V.V.S. Murthy, President of GITAM University on the Dias

One of Prof. Rao's classes in Tokyo

Shri Kishore Chandra Deo, Hon'ble Minister of Tribal and Panchayati Raj, Shri. B.L. Mungekar, former Member of Planning Commission, releasing the book *Gandhi and Applied Spirituality*

Greeting Shri Venkaiah Naidu, Vice-President of India

With his students later colleagues V. Bose and Pramila

With Dr. Roger D. Nelson (on the left), colleague at Princeton University, U.S.A.

Releasing the book *Elements of Parapsychology*

Releasing Prof. Rao's book *Colonial Syndrome*
by Shri Venkaiaha Naidu, Vice-President of India

With extended family

Bibliography of Publications

THIS IS A BIBLIOGRAPHY of my professional publications in English and some of their translations in languages such as German, Italian, Japanese, and Spanish. The publications are listed below chronologically from 1955 to date in two sections – books and papers.

Books

1957. *Psi Cognition.* Tenali: Tagore Publishing House.

1958. *Pre-university Logic.* Tenali: Tagore Publishing House.

1966. *Experimental Parapsychology: A Review and Interpretation.* Springfield: Charles C Thomas.

1967. *Parapsicologia Sperimentale: Esposizione & interpretazione.* Rome: Astrolabio.

1968. *Gandhi and Pragmatism: An Intercultural Study.* Calcutta: Oxford and IBH Publishing House.

1972. *Current Trends in Indian Philosophy* (ed. with K.S. Murthy). Visakhapatnam: Andhra University Press.

1972. *Mystic Awareness: Four Lectures on the Paranormal.* Mysore: Mysore University Press.

1973. *Experimental Studies of the Differential Effect in Life Setting* (with P. Sailaja). (Parapsychological Monographs, No. 13). New York: Parapsychology Foundation.

1982. *J.B. Rhine: On the Frontiers of Science* (ed.). Jefferson, NC: McFarland.

1984. *Basic Experiments in Parapsychology* (ed.). Jefferson, NC: McFarland.

1986. *Case Studies in Parapsychology* (ed.). Jefferson, NC: McFarland.

1993. *Cultivating Consciousness: Enhancing Human Potential, Wellness, and Healing* (ed.). Westport, CT: Praeger.

1994. *Charles Honorton and the Impoverished State of Skepticism: Essays on a Parapsychological Pioneer* (ed.). Jefferson, NC: McFarland.

2001. *Basic Research in Parapsychology* (ed.). Jefferson, NC: McFarland.

2002. *Consciousness Studies: Cross-cultural Perspectives.* Jefferson, NC: McFarland.

2005. *Towards a Spiritual Psychology* (ed. with S.B. Marwaha). New Delhi: Samvad (India).

2008. *Handbook of Indian Psychology* (ed. with A.C. Paranjpe and A.K. Dalal). Delhi: Foundation Books (Cambridge University Press).

2010. *Yoga and Parapsychology* (ed.). New Delhi: Motilal Banarsidass.

2010. *Violence, Identity and Gandhi.* Visakhapatnam: Center for Gandhian Studies, GITAM University.

2011. *Cognitive Anomalies, Consciousness and Yoga.* New Delhi: Centre for Studies of Civilizations and Matrix Publishers.

2011. *Gandhi and Applied Spirituality.* New Delhi: Indian Council of Philosophical Research and Matrix Publishers.

2014. *Cultivating Consciousness: An East–West Journey.* Visakhapatnam: GITAM University Press and New Delhi: D.K. Printworld.

2016. *Psychology in Indian Tradition* (with A.C. Paranjpe). New Delhi: Springer Publications and D.K. Printworld.

2017. *Gandhi's Dharma.* New Delhi: Oxford University Press.

2017. *Elements of Parapsychology*. Jefferson, NC: McFarland.

2017. *Foundations of Yoga Psychology*. New Delhi: Springer Publications.

2018. *Colonial Syndrome in Modern India: The Videshi Mindset in Modern India*. New Delhi: D.K. Printworld.

2018. *Phenomenology of Violence* (ed. with B. Sambasiva Prasad). 2 volumes. New Delhi: D.K. Printworld.

2018. *Patanjali's Yogasutra: A Psychological Study*. New Delhi: D.K. Printworld.

2019. *Why I Am an Indian and Other Essays*. New Delhi: D.K. Printworld.

2019. *Srimad Bhagavadgita: A Treatise on Counselling*. New Delhi: D.K. Printworld.

Papers

1955

Paranormal Cognition: An Essay in Survey of Evidence and Theories. MA (Hons) dissertation. Visakhapatnam: Andhra University.

Vedanta and the Modus Operandi of Paranormal Cognition. *The Philosophical Quarterly*, vol. 5.

1956

A Note on Jung's Conception of Psyche. *Proceedings of the Indian Philosophical Congress.*

1959

Towards a New Hypothesis. The Second Annual Convention of the Parapsychological Association. *Journal of Parapsychology*, 23: 288 [Abstract].

1961

A Note on the Report of the Library Committee to the University Grants Commission and the UGC Revision of

Salary Scales of Librarians in Universities and Colleges. *Indian Librarian,* 16: 69-72.

Consideration of Some Theories in Parapsychology. *Journal of Parapsychology*, 25: 32-54.

ESP Response to Preferred Targets as Compared to ESP Symbols. The Fourth Annual Convention of the Parapsychological Association. *Journal of Parapsychology*, 25: 279 [Abstract].

Library Development in India. *Library Quarterly*, 31: 135-53 [also published in *Indian Librarian*, 16: 73-97].

Philosophy of Librarianship. *Indian Librarian*, 16: 69-72.

Pragmatism and Practical Idealism. PhD dissertation. Visakhapatnam: Andhra University.

1962

A Report of a GESP Experiment Carried Out in an Indian Ashram with the Experimenter in the Role of "Sender" and Two Swamis as "Receivers", the Target Material Being Religious Pictures. The Fifth Annual Convention of the Parapsychological Association. *Journal of Parapsychology,* 26: 264 (Note).

Library Co-operation in the United States. *Indian Librarian*, 17: 19-21.

The Preferential Effect in ESP. *Journal of Parapsychology*, 26: 252-59.

The Story of the Nation and the New Republic. *Triveni*, July, pp. 136-48.

1963

Studies in the Preferential Effect I: Target Preference with Types of Targets Unknown. *Journal of Parapsychology*, 27: 23-32.

Studies in the Preferential Effect II: A Language ESP Test Involving Precognition and "Intervention". *Journal of Parapsychology*, 27: 147-60.

Studies in the Preferential Effect III: The Reversal Effect in Psi Preference. *Journal of Parapsychology*, 27: 242-51.

The Psychological Picture of Psi. *Research Journal of Philosophy and Social Sciences*, 1: 1-28.

1964

Studies in the Preferential Effect IV: The Role of Key Cards in Preferential Response Situations. *Journal of Parapsychology*, 28: 28-41.

The Differential Response in Three New Situations. *Journal of Parapsychology*, 28: 81-92.

Book review: *Five Years of Report of Seth Sohan Lal Memorial Institute of Parapsychology*, by S.C. Mukherjee. Sri Ganganagar (India): SSLMI Institute, 1962. *Journal of Parapsychology*, 28: 59-62.

Book review: *Mind and Consciousness in Experimental Parapsychology*, by R.H. Thouless. Cambridge: Cambridge University Press, 1963. *Journal of Parapsychology*, 28: 136-38.

1965

ESP and the Manifest Anxiety Scale. *Journal of Parapsychology*, 29: 12-18.

Social Psychology of Psi: Differential Response in a Competitive Situation. *Journal of Parapsychology*, 29: 295-96 [Abstract].

The Bidirectionality of Psi. *Journal of Parapsychology*, 29: 230-50. (Presidential address to the Eighth Annual Convention of the Parapsychological Association). [Also published in the *Proceedings of the Parapsychological Association,* 2: 37-59].

Book review: *Time Devoured: A Materialistic Discussion of Duration*, by E. Parsons. London: Allen and Unwin, 1964. *Journal of Parapsychology*, 29: 54-56.

Book review: *Biographical Dictionary of Parapsychology*, by H. Pleasants. New York: Helix, 1964. *Journal of Parapsychology*, 29: 57-58.

Book review: *Philosophy, Theosophy, Parapsychology: Some Essays on Diverse Subjects*, by J.J. Portman. Leyden: Sythott, 1965. *Journal of Parapsychology*, 29: 129-30.

1966

Die theorie J.B. Rhine's. *Sonderubruck aus Parapsichologie*. Sieten, 742-44. Darmstadt: Wissenschaftliche Buchgesellschaft.

1967

Dissonance Hypothesis and Some Incongruent ESP Results (with B.K. Kanthamani and P. Sailaja). *International Journal of Parapsychology*, 9: 128-33.

World views: A Psychological Analysis of the Problem of "One and Many". *Journal of the Indian Academy of Applied Psychology*, 4: 63-67.

Book review: *ESP in Life and Lab: Tracing Hidden Channels*, by L.E. Rhine. New York: Macmillan, 1967. *Journal of Parapsychology*, 31: 302-06.

1968

ESP and HSPQ Scores on Neuroticism (with B.K. Kanthamani and P. Sailaja) *Proceedings of the Parapsychological Association*, 5: 59-60.

ESP Scores Before and After a Scheduled Interview (with B.K. Kanthamani and P. Sailaja). *Proceedings of the Parapsychological Association*, 5: 57-59.

Psi in Communities and Other Interpersonal Situations in the Eastern World. In R. Cavanna (ed.), *Psi and Favorable States of Consciousness: Proceedings of an International Conference on Methodology in Psi Research* (pp. 74-83). New York: Parapsychology Foundation.

Spontaneous ESP in Laboratory Tests: The Error Phenomena. *Journal of the American Society for Psychical Research*, 62: 63-72.

The Bearing of Yoga Practice on Psi Research. In R. Cavanna and M. Ullman (eds), *Psi and Altered States of Consciousness: Proceedings of an International Conference on Hypnosis, Drugs, Dreams, and Psi* (pp. 132-34). New York: Parapsychology Foundation.

1970

Book review: *Extrasensory Perception*, by G. Schmeidler. New York: Atherton Press, 1969. *Journal of the American Society for Psychical Research*, 64: 443-49.

1971

Humanities and the University. *Proceedings of the Symposium on Teaching of Humanities* (pp. 9-23). Waltair: Andhra University Press.

Personality Characteristics of ESP Subjects I: Primary Personality Characteristics and ESP (with B.K. Kanthamani). *Journal of Parapsychology*, 35: 189-207.

Teaching of Psychology in Indian Universities. *Proceedings of the Symposium on Teaching of Social Sciences* (pp. 62-77). Visakhapatnam: Andhra University Press.

Book review: *Dream Studies and Telepathy: An Experimental Approach*, by M. Ullman and S. Krippner (Parapsychological Monographs, No. 12). New York: Parapsychology Foundation, 1970. *Journal of the American Society for Psychical Research*, pp. 364-68.

1972

Alpha Rhythm and ESP in a Free-response Situation (with José Feola). In W.G. Roll, R.L. Morris, and J.D. Morris (eds), *Research in Parapsychology*, 1971 (pp. 141-44). Metuchen, NJ: Scarecrow Press.

Consciousness in Indian Psychology. Paper presented at the Third International Conference on Humanistic Psychology, Tokyo.

Education for Living and Learning. (First Convocation Address given at V.S.R. College). Tenali: V.S.R. College.

Personality Characteristics of ESP Subjects II: The Combined Personality Measure (CPM) and ESP (with H. Kanthamani). *Journal of Parapsychology*, 36: 56-70.

Personality Characteristics of ESP Subjects III: Extraversion and ESP (with H. Kanthamani). *Journal of Parapsychology*, 36: 198-212.

Practicalistic Approach to Philosophy. In K.S. Murthy and K.R. Rao (eds), *Current Trends in Indian Philosophy* (pp. 259-68). Waltair: Andhra University Press.

1973

Koneru Ramakrishna Rao: An Autobiographical Note. *Parapsych Review*, July-August, 4(4): 13-15.

Beyond the Five Senses. *Science Today*, June, pp. 27-34.

Meditation and ESP Scoring (with Hamlyn Dukhan). In W.G. Roll, R.L. Morris, and J.D. Morris (eds), *Research in Parapsychology,* 1972 (pp. 148-51). Metuchen, NJ: Scarecrow Press.

Modernization: An Adaptation Process. Paper presented at the seminar on "The Ethos of Development and the Role of Religion". Visakhapatnam: Andhra University.

Personality Characteristics of ESP Subjects IV: Neuroticism and ESP (with H. Kanthamani). *Journal of Parapsychology*, 37: 37-50.

Book review: *Reincarnation and Science*, by R. Reyna. New Delhi: Sterling Publishers, 1973. *Journal of Parapsychology*, 39: 262-64.

Personality Characteristics of ESP Subjects V: Graphic Expansiveness and ESP (with H. Kanthamani). *Journal of Parapsychology*, 37: 119-29.

Psi, Science and Society: A Change in Methodology Is Needed. In W.G. Roll, R.L. Morris, and J.D. Morris (eds), *Research in Parapsychology,* 1972 (pp. 107-10). Metuchen, NJ: Scarecrow Press.

Some Reflections on Examinations. Paper presented at the seminar on "Examinations in Higher Education". Hyderabad: The State Council of Educational Research and Training.

The Role of Test Preparedness in Psi Experiments (with P. Sailaja). In W.G. Roll, R.L. Morris, and J.D. Morris (eds),

Research in Parapsychology, 1972 (pp. 151-53). Metuchen, NJ: Scarecrow Press.

1974

Concerning Man and Modernity. (Second Convocation Address given at Bapatla College of Arts and Science on 2 February). Bapatla: Bapatla College of Arts and Science.

Indian Psychology: Dreaming. *Proceedings of the Fifth Annual Conference on Humanistic Psychology*. Visakhapatnam: Andhra University, Department of Psychology and Parapsychology, p. 37 [Abstract].

Psi and Personality. In John Beloff (ed.), *New Directions in Parapsychology* (pp. 60-76). London: Elek Science.

Social Conflict: Some Crucial Issues. (Paper presented at the Fifteenth All-India Seminar on Philosophy and Social Conflict). Madras: Centre for Advanced Study in Philosophy, University of Madras.

Whither Examinations? (Convocation Address given at Government College on 17 April). Srikakulam: Government College.

Book review: *Parapsychology: Sources of Information*, by R.A. White and L.A. Dale, Metuchen, NJ: Scarecrow Press, 1973. *Journal of Parapsychology*, 38: 247-49.

1975

Consciousness in Indian Psychology. (Paper presented at the Eighteenth All-India Seminar on the Concept of Consciousness). Madras: Centre for the Advanced Study in Philosophy, University of Madras.

Introduction. In S. Krippner, *Song of the Siren: A Parapsychological Odyssey* (pp. xv-xvii). New York: Harper & Row.

Psi and Yoga Psychology. *ASPR Newsletter*, 27 (autumn).

The Psyche and Soma in Indian Psychology. In L. Pozzi (ed.), *Proceedings of the Third International Congress on Therapy in Psychosomatic Medicine* (pp. 70-77). Rome: International College of Psychosomatic Medicine.

Book review: *Transpersonal Psychologies*, by C.T. Tart. New York: Harper and Row, 1975. *Journal of Parapsychology*, 39: 262-64.

1976

Interview (with Alan Vaughan). *Psychic*, 7(4): 48-54.

Teaching of Parapsychology in India and the Andhra Experiment. In B. Shapin and L. Coly (eds), *Proceedings of the Twenty-Fourth International Conference on Education in Parapsychology* (pp. 108-23). New York: Parapsychology Foundation. Also in *Parapsychology Review*, 7: 1-8.

1977

ESP in Life Situations: An Attempted Replication (with D.H. Weiner). *Journal of Parapsychology*, 41: 157-58 [Abstract].

Paired-associates Recall and ESP: A Study of Memory and Psi-missing (with M. Morrison and J.W. Davis). *The Journal of Parapsychology*, 41(3): 166-86.

ESP Testing in Life Situations: A Cross-cultural Study of Psi in Academic Examinations (with J.T. Obrien). *Journal of Parapsychology*, 41: 1-9.

Mental Imagery and ESP as Measured by Rao's Subsensory Psi Test (SPT) (with R. Vindhya Rao and P.V. Krishna Rao). In J.D. Morris, W.G. Roll, and R.L. Morris (eds), *Research in Parapsychology*, 1976 (pp. 105-07). Metuchen, NJ: Scarecrow Press.

Some Frustrations and Challenges in Parapsychology. *Journal of Parapsychology*, 41(2): 119-35.

Subsensory Perception (SSP), Extrasensory Perception (ESP) and Meditation (with I. Puri). In J.D. Morris, W.G. Roll, and R.L. Morries (eds), *Research in Parapsychology*, 1976 (pp. 7-9). Metuchen, NJ: Scarecrow Press.

The Role of Association in Memory-recall and ESP (with M. Morrison, J.W. Davis, and J.A. Freeman). *Journal of Parapsychology*, 41: 190-97.

Book review: *The Philosophy of Parapsychology*, ed. by B. Shapin and L. Coly. New York: Parapsychology Foundation, 1977. *Journal of Parapsychology*, 41: 215-19.

Book review: *Handbook of Parapsychology*, by B.B. Wolman. New York: Van Nostrand and Reinhold, 1977. *Journal of Parapsychology*, 41: 352-58.

On the Nature of Psi: An Examination of Some Attempts to Explain ESP and PK (reprint). *Journal of Parapsychology*, 41(4): 294-351.

1978

Electrical Activity of the Brain and ESP: An Exploratory Study (with J. Feola). *Journal of Indian Psychology*, 2: 118-33.

Expectancy Effects, ESP Effects and Replicability. *The Behavioral and Brain Sciences*, 3: 403-04.

Further Studies of Memory and ESP. *Journal of Parapsychology*, 42: 167-78.

Psi and Its Place in Nature. (Presidential Address, 21st Annual Convention of the Parapsychological Association.) *Journal of Parapsychology*, 42: 276-303. Also in W.G. Roll (ed.), *Research in Parapsychology,* 1978 (pp. 159-83). Metuchen, NJ: Scarecrow Press.

Psychology of Transcendence: A Study in Early Buddhistic Psychology. *Journal of Indian Psychology*, 1(1): 1-21.

Review of Recent Books on Hypnosis. *Journal of Indian Psychology*, 1(2): 222-24.

Subsensory Perception (SSP), Extrasensory Perception (ESP) and Transcendental Meditation (TM) (with I. Puri). *Journal of Indian Psychology*, 1(1): 69-74.

The Differential Effect and Experimenter Effects in Intentional and Non-intentional Psi Tests (with J.W. Davis). *Journal of Parapsychology*, 42: 1-19.

The Role of Association in Memory-recall and ESP (with M. Morrison, J.W. Davis, and J.A. Freeman). In W.G. Roll (ed.), *Research in Parapsychology,* 1977 (pp. 84-90). Metuchen, NJ: Scarecrow Press.

Book review: *Philosophical Dimensions of Parapsychology*, ed. by J.M.O. Wheatley and H. Edge. Springfield, IL: Charles C. Thomas, 1976. *Journal of Indian Psychology*, 1(1): 81-82.

Book review: *Philosophy and Parapsychology*, by J. Ludwig. Buffalo: Prometheus, 1978. *Journal of Parapsychology*, 42: 319-21.

Book review: *Philosophy and Psychical Research*, by S.C. Thakur. New York: Humanities Press, 1976. *Journal of Indian Psychology*, 1: 69-74.

Yogic Meditation and Psi Scoring in Forced-choice and Free-response Tests (with H. Dukhan and P.V. Krishna Rao) (reprint). *Journal of Indian Psychology*, 1(2): 160-75.

1979

The Institute for Parapsychology. *PSI News. Parapsychological Association*, 2(2).

Imagery, Concreteness, and Meaningfulness of Target Words in Relation to Psi Scoring: A Preliminary Experiment (with H. Kanthamani). *Journal of Parapsychology*, 43: 46-47 [Abstract].

Language ESP Tests under Normal and Relaxed Conditions. *Journal of Parapsychology*, 43: 1-15.

Language ESP Tests with a Single Subject under Normal and Relaxed Conditions. In W.G. Roll (ed.), *Research in Parapsychology,* 1978 (pp. 90-91). Metuchen, NJ: Scarecrow Press.

On "The Scientific Credibility of ESP". *Perceptual and Motor Skills*, 49: 415-29.

Psi and Volitional Activity: An Experimental Study of Psi in a Competitive Situation (with H. Kanthamani and S.R. Krishna). *Journal of Parapsychology*, 43: 101-12.

Where Have We Gone Wrong? *Journal of Parapsychology*, 43: 48-49 [Abstract].

Book review: *The Reception of Unconventional Science*, by S.H. Mauskopf. AAAS Selected Symposium 25. Boulder, CO: Westview Press, 1979. *Journal of Parapsychology*, 43: 241-43.

1980

ESP Tests with Competition Set: Further Explorations of Volitional Influence on Psi (with H. Kanthamani). *Journal of Parapsychology*, 44: 341-52.

Exploratory Free-response Studies with Maimonides Slides (with R.J. Munson). *Journal of Parapsychology*, 44: 78 [Abstract].

Further Studies of Psi and Volitional Activity (with H. Kanthamani). In W.G. Roll (ed.), *Research in Parapsychology*, pp. 115-18. Metuchen, NJ: Scarecrow Press.

Seven Evidential Experiments: A Commentary on Dr. Beloff's Paper. *Zetetic Scholar*, issue 6: 107-09.

"Signs of Psi" in Two Series of Long-distance Experiments with a Single Subject (with H. Kanthamani). *Journal of Parapsychology*, 44: 63-64. [Abstract].

1981

A Tribute to J.B. Rhine. *Journal of the American Society for Psychical Research*, 75: 71-72.

Hume's Fallacy. *Journal of Parapsychology*, 45: 147-52.

On the Question of Replication. *Journal of Parapsychology*, 45: 311-20.

Personality and "Belief" in Relation to Language ESP Scores (with S.R. Krishna). In W.G. Roll and J. Beloff (eds), *Research in Parapsychology*, 1980 (pp. 61-63). Metuchen, NJ: Scarecrow Press.

Possible Sex Related Differences in ESP Scoring of the Same and Opposite Sex Pairs in Competition/Cooperation Situations. *Journal of Indian Psychology*, 3(2): 41-51.

Subliminal Perception and Extrasensory Perception in a Learning Paradigm (with R.J. Munson). In W.G. Roll and J. Beloff (eds), *Research in Parapsychology*, 1980 (pp. 96-98). Metuchen, NJ: Scarecrow Press.

The Volitional Effect in Competition and Cooperation Situations (with S.R. Krishna and H. Kanthamani). *Journal of Indian Psychology*, 3(1): 47-56.

1982

An Attempted Replication of Sex Differences in Volitional Studies (with B. Norwood). In W.G. Roll, J. Beloff, and R.A. White (eds), *Research in Parapsychology,* 1981 (pp. 200-201). Metuchen, NJ: Scarecrow Press.

J.B. Rhine and His Critics. Introduction. In K.R. Rao (ed.), *J.B. Rhine: On the Frontiers of Science: The Life and Work of J.B. Rhine* (pp. 192-212). Jefferson, NC: McFarland.

Memory and ESP: An Attempted Replication (with D. Weiner). *Journal of Parapsychology*, 46: 56 [Abstract].

Possible Sex-related Differences in ESP Scoring of Same- and Opposite-sex Pairs in Competition/Cooperation Experiments. In W.G. Roll, R.L. Morris, and R.A. White (eds), *Research in Parapsychology,* 1981 (pp. 154-65). Metuchen, NJ: Scarecrow Press.

Science and the Legitimacy of Psi. In B. Shapin and L. Coly (eds), *Parapsychology and the Experimental Method* (pp. 100-112). New York: Parapsychology Foundation.

The a priori and Theoretical Objections to Psi. *Journal of Indian Psychology*, 4(1): 3-12.

Two Studies of ESP and Subliminal Perception (with P.V. Krishna Rao). *Journal of Parapsychology*, 46: 185-208.

1983

From Proof to Acceptance. *Parapsychology Review*, 14(2): 1-3.

ESP and SP in TM and non-TM Groups (with P.V.K. Rao). In W.G. Roll, J. Beloff, and R.A. White (eds), *Research in Parapsychology,* 1982 (pp. 189-90). Metuchen, NJ: Scarecrow Press.

L.E. Rhine on Psi and Its Place. *Journal of Parapsychology*, 47: 347-60.

On the Question of Application. In W.G. Roll, J. Beloff, and R.A. White (eds). *Research in Parapsychology*, 1982 (pp. 263-64). Metuchen, NJ: Scarecrow Press.

Sex Related Differential Scoring in Two Volitional Studies (with H. Kanthamani and B. Norwood). *Journal of Parapsychology*, 43: 7-22.

The Volitional Effect in Blind-matching ESP Tests (with S.R. Krishna). *Journal of Parapsychology*, 47: 51-52 [Abstract].

Two Series of Volitional Studies with Competition Set (with C. Sargent and M.J. Schlitz). In W.G. Roll, J. Beloff, and R.A. White (eds), *Research in Parapsychology,* 1982 (pp. 190-93). Metuchen, NJ: Scarecrow Press.

Book review: *Psychical Research: A Guide to Its History, Principles and Practices*, ed. by I. Grattan-Guiness. Wellingborough: Aquarian Press, 1982. *Journal of the Society for Psychical Research*, 52: 135-37.

Book review: *Psychology's Occult Doubles: Psychology and the Problem of Pseudoscience*, by T.H. Leahey and G.E. Leahey. Chicago: Nelson-Hall, 1983. *Journal of Parapsychology*, 47: 274-75.

1984

Introduction. In K.R. Rao (ed.), *The Basic Experiments in Parapsychology* (pp. 1-11). Jefferson, NC: McFarland.

Parapsychology. In R.J. Corsini (ed.), *Encyclopedia of Psychology* (vol. 2, pp. 478-82). New York: John Wiley.

Parapsychology: Implications for Religion and Science. Paper presented at the Isthmus Institute, Dallas, Texas.

Rhine, Joseph Banks (1895-1980). In R.J. Corsini (ed.), *Encyclopedia of Psychology* (vol. 3, p. 239). New York: John Wiley.

The Ganzfeld Debate: Introduction. *Journal of Parapsychology*, 49: 1-2.

Book review: *The Encyclopedic Dictionary of Psychology* by R. Harre and R. Lamb. Cambridge, MA: MIT Press, 1983. *Journal of Parapsychology*, 48: 234-35.

Book review: *Test Your ESP Potential: A Complete Kit with Institutions. Scorecards, and Apparatus*, by James Randi. New

York: Dower Publications. *Journal of Parapsychology*, 48: 353-55.

1985

Replications in Conventional and Controversial Sciences. In B. Shapin and L. Coly (eds), *The Repeatability Problem in Parapsychology* (pp. 23-24). New York: Parapsychology Foundation.

1986

Case Studies in Parapsychology: Papers presented in honor of Dr. Louisa E. Rhine at a conference held on 12 November 1983 at Bryan University Center, Duke University, Durham, North Carolina. Jefferson, NC: McFarland.

L.E. Rhine on Psi and Its Place. In K.R. Rao (ed.), *Case Studies in Parapsychology* (pp. 52-62). Jefferson, NC: McFarland.

Louisa E. Rhine: 1891-1983. In K.R. Rao (ed.), *Case Studies in Parapsychology* (pp. 1-5). Jefferson, NC: McFarland.

Toward Reorganizing Higher Education in the State (with others), Report. Hyderabad, AP: Government of Andhra Pradesh.

Parapsychology: Implications of Religion and Science (reprint). *Perkins Journal.* April, 39:1.

1987

India's Heritage: A Philosophical Rendezvous. Gurubhaktha Ratna Sri Polisetty Seetharamanjaneyulu: Memorial Lecture, Nagarjuna Nagar, Acharya Nagarjuna University.

Journal of Parapsychology: The First and the Next Fifty Years. *Journal of Parapsychology*, 51: 1-8.

Parapsychology. In Raymond Corsini (ed.), *Concise Encyclopedia of Psychology* (pp. 800-802). New York: John Wiley.

Rhine, J.B. In Raymond Corsini (ed.), *Concise Encyclopedia of Psychology* (p. 985). New York: John Wiley.

The Anomaly Called Psi: Recent Research and Criticism (with J. Palmer). *Behavioral and Brain Sciences*, 10: 539-51.

The Institute for Professional Studies (with others), Report. Hyderabad, AP: Government of Andhra Pradesh.

Where Lies the Bias? (with J. Palmer). *Behavioral and Brain Sciences*, 10: 618-27.

Book review: *Foundations of Parapsychology: Exploring the Boundaries of Human Capability*, by H.L. Edge, R.L. Morris, J.H. Rush, and J.A. Palmer. Boston, MA: Routledge and Kegan Paul, 1986. *Journal of Parapsychology*, 51: 353-57.

1988

Are We Throwing the Baby Out with the Bath Water? In L. Coly, D.S. Joanne and M.C. Mahon (eds), *Psi Research Methodology*. New York: Parapsychology Foundation.

Editorial : Joseph Greenwood. *Journal of Parapsychology*, 52: 95-97.

Psychology of Transcendence: A Study in Early Buddhistic Psychology. In A.C. Paranjpe, D.G.F. Ho, and R.W. Riebu (eds), *Asian Contributions to Psychology* (pp. 123-48). New York: Praeger.

Report of the Committee on Establishing a Rural University in Andhra Pradesh (with others). Hyderabad, AP: Department of Education, Government of Andhra Pradesh.

What Is Indian Psychology? *Journal of Indian Psychology*, 7(1): 37-57.

What Is Indian Psychology? Presidential Address delivered on 25 February, *The Twenty Fifth Annual Conference of the Indian Academy of Applied Psychology*, Hyderabad: Osmania University.

Book review: *Concise Encyclopedia of Psychology*, by R.J. Corsini. New York: John Wiley, 1987. *Journal of Parapsychology*, 52: 83-84.

Book review: *Jung*: *A Biography*, by G. Wehr. Boston, MA: Shambala, 1987. *Journal of Parapsychology*, 52: 82-83.

Books in brief. *Journal of Parapsychology*, 52: 82-85.

Books in brief. *Journal of Parapsychology*, 52: 241-45.

1989

Meditation Secular and Sacred – A Review and Assessment of Some Recent Research. *Journal of the Indian Academy of Applied Psychology*, 15(2): 51-75.

Meditation Secular and Sacred: A Review and Assessment of Current Scientific Research, Presidential Address, Calcutta: University of Calcutta.

1990

Exploring Normal–Paranormal Interaction within a Memory–ESP Testing Paradigm (with H. Kanthamani). In A. Henkel and J. Palmer (eds). *Research in Parapsychology,* 1989 (pp. 62-67). Metuchen, NJ: The Scarecrow Press.

Heretical Psychology: On the Scope and Substance of Psychical Research. In A.H. Linda and R.S. Gertrude (eds), *Proceedings of the Parapsychological Association,* Metuchen, NJ: The Scarecrow Press.

Psychology, the Psychoid and Parapsychology (interview with S.A. Martin). *Quadrant*, 24: 11-23.

Foreword. In I.V. Chalapati Rao. *Sankara: Humanist, Integrator, Poet and Philosopher* (pp.ix-xvi). Hyderabad: Telugu University.

1991

Afterword. In H. Motoyama. *The Correlation Between Psi Energy and Ki.* Tokyo: Human Science Press.

Consciousness Research and Psi. *Journal of Parapsychology*, 55: 1-43.

Effect of ESP Feedback on Subject's Responses to a Personality Questionnaire (with S.R. Krishna). *Journal of Parapsychology*, 55: 147-58.

Exploring Normal–Paranormal Interaction within a Memory–ESP Testing Paradigm (with H. Kanthamani and John Palmer). *Journal of Parapsychology*, 54: 245-59.

Healing, Meditation, and Anomalous Mental Phenomena. *Journal of Indian Psychology*, 9: 1-13.

Introduction. *The Legacy of L.E. Rhine: A Panel Discussion to Commemorate LER'S Birth Centenary.*

Skeptics and Selective Reporting. *Contemporary Psychology*, 36(11): 1013-14.

1992

Early History of the Paranormal: An Essay Review of Brain Inglis's *Natural and Supernatural. Journal of Parapsychology*, 56: 147-62.

Meditation and Mind/Matter Interface. In B. Rubik (ed.), *The Interrelationship between Mind and Matter* (pp. 111-41). Philadelphia, PA: Center for Frontier Sciences, Temple University.

The Two Sides of Psi Debate. *Contemporary Psychology*, 37: 1106-08.

1993

Charles Honorton: A Man of Many Talents. *Journal of the American Society for Psychical Research*, 87: 356-58.

Charles Honorton: A Savant of His Own Kind. *Journal of Parapsychology*, 57: 1-6.

Consciousness, Awareness, and First-person Perspective. *Behavioral and Brain Sciences*, 16: 407-09.

Cultivating Consciousness: Some Conceptual and Methodological Issues. In K.R. Rao (ed.), *Cultivating Consciousness* (pp. 82-100). Westport, CT: Praeger.

C.T.K. Chari (1908-1993). *Journal of the Society for Psychical Research*, 59: 237-40.

Demonstration Research and Meta-analysis in Parapsychology (with S. Krippner, W. Braud, I.L. Child, J. Palmer, M. Schlitz, R. White, and J. Utts). *Journal of Parapsychology*, 57: 275-86.

Exploring Consciousness: Some Conceptual and Methodological Issues. Paper presented at the Third International Symposium on Consciousness and Science, 2-6 January 1993, Olympia, Greece.

Karma, Reincarnation and Parapsychology. Paper presented at the Conference on Karma, Reincarnation and Past Life Therapy, 18-19 September 1993, California Institute for Human Sciences.

Parapsychology and Religion. Paper presented at the Parliament of World Religions, 2 September 1993, Chicago.

1994

Consciousness. In R.J. Corsini (ed.), *Encyclopedia of Psychology* (2nd edn, vol. 1, pp. 302-06). New York: John Wiley.

Introduction. In K.R. Rao (ed.), *Charles Honorton and the Impoverished State of Skepticism: Essays on a Parapsychological Pioneer* (pp. 1-6). Jefferson, NC: McFarland.

Parapsychology. In R.J. Corsini (ed.). *Encyclopedia of Psychology* (2nd edn, vol. 3, pp. 10-15). New York: John Wiley.

Anomalies of Consciousness: Indian Perspectives and Research. *The Journal of Parapsychology*, 58: 149-87.

1995

Human Rights and Social Identity: A Gandhian Perspective. Lecture at the Centre for Studies in Human Rights and Social Development. Tirupati: S.V. University.

Reforming School Education, (with others) Committee Report. Hyderabad, AP: Government of Andhra Pradesh.

Some Reflections on Religion and Anomalies of Consciousness. *Journal of Indian Psychology*, 13: 1-15. [Also published in *Reviews*, 18(1): 11-18].

1996

Why Am I an Indian?: Reflections on Indian Identity and National Integration. In K.S. Murthy and A. Dasgupta (eds), *The Perennial Tree* (pp. 354-78). New Delhi: New Age International.

1997

Some Reflections on Religion and Anomalies of Consciousness. In Charles T. Tart (ed.), *Body, Mind, Spirit* (pp. 68-83).

Newburyport, MA: Hampton Roads Publishing.

1998

Two Faces of Consciousness : A Look at Eastern and Western Perspectives. *Journal of Consciousness Studies*, 5(3): 309-27.

1999

Does ESP Exist? *CIHS Newsletter*, 6: 3-4.

2000

Higher Education in India: Ground 00 and Vision 2020. (Dr. Sarvepalli Radhakrishnan Memorial Lecture). Visakhapatnam: Andhra University Press.

2001

Consciousness Studies: A Survey of Perspectives and Research. In J. Pandey (ed.), *Psychology in India Revisited: Developments in the Discipline* (pp. 19-62). New Delhi: Sage Publications.

Introduction: Reality, Replicability and Lawfulness of Psi. In K.R. Rao (ed.), *Basic Research in Parapsychology* (pp. 3-37). Jefferson, NC: McFarland.

Psi and Self. In P. Howell and J. Hall (eds), *Self Through Art and Science* (pp. 175-89). Bloomington, IN: 1st Books Library.

2002

Bridging Eastern and Western Perspectives on Consciousness. *Journal of Consciousness Studies*, 9(11): 63-68.

Perception, Cognition and Consciousness in Classical Indian Psychology. Keynote address, National Workshop on *Puzzles of Perception*, Department of Psychology, University of Delhi and Indian Council of Philosophical Research, 14-16 March.

2003

Prolegomena to Indian Psychology Book Project. In *Indian Psychology Book Project Meeting* sponsored by the Infinity Foundation and the Institute for Human Science and Service (pp. 8-44). Visakhapatnam: Institute for Human Science and Service.

2004

Brain, Mind and Consciousness. *The Theosophist*, 125: 291-99.

Centrality of Consciousness in Indian Psychology. In Kireet Joshi and Matthijs Cornellissen (eds), *Consciousness, Indian Psychology and Yoga* (pp. 53-75). New Delhi: PHISPC, Centre for Studies in Civilizations.

Classical Indian Psychology: Lessons for Education, Health and Wellness. In *Work Culture and Efficiency with Special Reference to Indriyas*. D. Prahladchari (Chief Editor) and M.L. Narasimha Murty and Rani Sadisiva Murty (eds) (pp. 27-33). Tirupathi: Rashtriya Sanskrit Vidyapeetha.

Knowing and Being: Exploring the Cross-cultural Contours of Consciousness Studies. In Sangeetha Menon et al. (eds), *Science and Beyond: Cosmology, Consciousness and Technology in the Indic Traditions* (pp. 155-80). Bangalore: National Institute of Advanced Studies.

Long Journey and Lone Memories. In George Victor (ed.), *Philosophical Tradition and Unified Curriculum: Profiles, Perspectives and Syllabus*. New Delhi: D.K. Printworld.

2005

Introduction. In K. Ramakrishna Rao and Sonali Bhatt Marwaha (eds), *Towards a Spiritual Psychology: Essays in Indian Psychology* (pp. 1-17). New Delhi: Samvad India Foundation.

Perception, Cognition and Consciousness in Classical Hindu Psychology. *Journal of Consciousness Studies*, 12(3): 3-30.

Religiosity and Sense of Well-being: Spiritual Dimensions of Health. In A.K. Dalal and S. Ray (eds), *Social Dimensions of Health* (pp. 69-88). Jaipur: Rawat Publications.

Scope and Substance of Indian Psychology. In K.R. Rao and S.B. Marwaha (ed.), *Towards a Spiritual Psychology: Essays in Indian Psychology* (pp. 18-40). New Delhi: Samvad (India).

2006

Philosophy of Identity: From Personal to Global Human Identity. Invited Address at the Symposium, *Is Philosophy*

Regional or Global ? 17 December 2006, Interim World Philosophy Congress, University of Delhi.

A Plea for Promoting Indigenous Cognitive Psychology in India. 2nd International Conference on Cognitive Science, Allahabad, 10-12 December 2006.

A Study of the Relationship between Religion, Personality and the Paranormal. National Conference, Training-cum-Workshop, Andhra University, Visakhapatnam, 3-23 January 2006.

An Investigation of Cognitive Anomalies among College Students. National Conference, Training-cum-Workshop, Visakhapatnam, 3-23 January 2006.

Bharatiya-Jiva-Sastra-Sutra (Principles of Indian Psychology). Inaugural Address, National Seminar on Holistic Paradigms in Psychology: Problems and Prospects. New Delhi: Zakir Husain College.

Consciousness and Cognitive Anomalies. In Sangeetha Menon (ed.), *Consciousness, Experience and Ways of Knowing* (pp. 41-101). Bangalore: National Institute of Advanced Studies.

The Relevance of Philosophy to Life in the 21st Century. International Conference on Relevance of Philosophy to Life in the 21st Century, Colombo, 21 November 2006. *Sri Lanka Journal of Social Sciences*, 29/30 (1&2): 13-41.

Theories of Self/Person in Classical Indian Thought. Keynote Address, UGC National Seminar on Relevance of Philosophy in 21st Century, Visakhapatnam: Andhra University, 27 January 2006.

2007

A Brief Introduction to Indian Psychology. UGC National Seminar cum Workshop, St. Joseph's College of Education, November 2007, Guntur.

Identity and Inclusiveness in Gautama Buddha's Social Philosophy. International Conference on Buddhism, 3-5 February 2007, Bodh Gaya, Bihar.

Indian Psychology Panel Discussion. National Seminar on Indian Psychology: Theories and Models, 26-28 December 2007, VYASA University, Bangalore.

Is Indian Psychology Positive? National Conference on Positive Psychology, 28-29 February 2007. Chandigarh: Punjab University.

Meditating on the Mandala of Indian Identity. Paper presented at the National Workshop on National Integration and Multiple Identities, 15 September 2007, Shimla: Indian Institute of Advanced Studies. *Journal of Indian Council of Philosophical Research*, 24: 33-65.

Principles of Yoga Psychology. Conference on Meditation and Spirituality: Scientific, Conceptual, and Applied Perspectives. Center for Study of Health, Religion and Spirituality, Indiana State University, Terre Haute, Indiana.

The Intellectual Legacy of Jawaharlal Nehru. Keynote Address, National Seminar on Jawaharlal Nehru's Philosophy, Policies and Performance: Reflections, Retrospect and Prospects, 3-5 April 2007, Guntur: Acharya Nagarjuna University.

The Legacy and Relevance of Lord Buddha. National Seminar on Lord Buddha and His Universe, 29-30 March 2007, Shimla: Indian Institute of Advanced Study.

Towards an Inclusive Psychology with Indian Identity. Editorial Conclave, Project of History of Indian Science, Philosophy and Culture, 2 April 2007, New Delhi.

Yoga-Advaita Psychology: An Inclusive Psychology for the Future. 17th International Congress on Vedanta, 23 September 2007, Oxford, OH: Miami University.

2008

Buddhist Psychology: Phenomenology of Consciousness. Fifth International Buddhist Conference, 10 January 2008, K.J. Somaiya Centre for Buddhist Studies, Mumbai.

Introducing Indian Psychology. In K.R. Rao, A.C. Paranjpe, and A.K. Dalal (eds), *Handbook of Indian Psychology* (pp. 1-18).

Delhi: Foundation Books (Cambridge University Press).

Psychology in the Advaita Vedanta (with A.C. Paranjpe). In K.R. Rao, A.C. Paranjpe, and A.K. Dalal (eds), *Handbook of Indian Psychology* (pp. 253-85). Delhi: Foundation Books (Cambridge University Press).

Taxonomy of Consciousness. In N. Srinivasan, A.K. Gupta, and J. Pandey (eds), *Advances in Cognitive Science* (vol. 1, pp. 383-423). New Delhi: Sage.

Yoga Psychology: Theory and Application (with A.C. Paranjpe). In K.R. Rao, A.C. Paranjpe, and A.K. Dalal (eds), *Handbook of Indian Psychology* (pp. 186-216). Delhi: Foundation Books (Cambridge University Press).

2009

Centrality of Consciousness: The BMC Model of the Person (Patanjali Lecture). Dartmouth, MA: University of Massachusetts.

Road Map to Reform Higher Education: From Radhakrishnan Commission Report to Yashpal Committee Recommendations. Indo-French Joint Seminar on Challenges in Public Higher Education, 21 December 2009. New Delhi: Indian Council of Social Sciences Research.

Science and Spirituality: In Search of a Common Ground. Presidential Address, Conference on Science and Spirituality, 4 April 2009, Kolkata: Ramakrishna Mission Institute of Culture.

Violence: A Philosophical Rendezvous. (Extracts from the Keynote Address at National Workshop on National Integration and Identity Violence, North Eastern Hill University, Shillong, 20-23 March 2009. *ICPR Newsletter* (October 2008–March 2009): 1-6.

Yoga Psychology: Towards a Psychology of the Future, Lecture at University of Massachusetts, Dartmouth, 30 April 2009.

2010

Asian Philosophies in Search of Identity. Presidential Address,

1st Asian Philosophy Congress, 6-9 March 2010. New Delhi: Jawaharlal Nehru University. *ICPR Newsletter* (January–March): 3-5.

Cognitive Anomalies: Developing Tests for Screening and Selecting Subjects. In K.R. Rao (ed.), *Yoga and Parapsychology* (pp. 393-426). Delhi: Motilal Banarsidass.

Violence, Identity and Gandhi. National Seminar on Current Scenes of Conflict: Gandhian Perspectives for Resolution, 19-21 March 2010. New Delhi: Indian Council of Philosophical Research and Visakhapatnam: GITAM University.

Indian Psychology: Towards a Psychology of the Future. In D.K. Bhattacharjee (ed.), *Psychology and Education: Indian Perspectives* (pp. 5-33). New Delhi: Indian Council of Educational Research and Training.

Paranormal Phenomena and Yoga Psychology and Practice. National Seminar on Parapsychology: From Indian Philosophical Perspectives, 4-5 January 2010. Visakhapatnam: Department of Psychology and Parapsychology, Andhra University.

Parapsychology and Yoga. In K.R. Rao (ed.), *Yoga and Parapsychology* (pp. 1-41). Delhi: Motilal Banarsidass.

Spirituality and Science of Consciousness. International Seminar on Spirituality and Science of Consciousness, 8 January 2010, Kolkata: Ramakrishna Mission Institute of Culture.

The Question of Post-mortem Survival: Empirical Evidence and Theoretical Issues. In K.R. Rao (ed.), *Yoga and Parapsychology* (pp. 261-300). Delhi: Motilal Banarsidass.

2011

Applied Yoga Philosophy: Studies of Neurophysiology of Meditation. *Journal of Consciousness Studies*, 18(11-12): 161-98.

Hypnosis, Yoga and Psychic Phenomena. In R. Sharma and B.M. Palan (eds), *Hypnosis: Psycho-philosophical Perspectives and Therapeutic Relevance* (pp. 3-31). New Delhi: Concept Publishing Company.

Indian Psychology: Implications and Applications. In R.M.M. Cornelissen, Y. Misra, and S. Varma (eds) *Foundations of Indian Psychology: Theories and Concepts* (vol. 1, pp. 7-26). Delhi: Longman Pearson.

Keynote address. In *Spirituality and Science of Consciousness* (pp. 14-63). Kolkata: Ramakrishna Mission Institute of Culture.

Triśūla: Trident Model of Person in Indian Psychology. In Girishwar Misra (ed.), *Handbook of Psychology in India* (pp. 17-35). New Delhi: Oxford University Press.

Violence and Nonviolence in Gandhi's Philosophy of Life (October–December 2011). *GITAM Journal of Gandhian Studies*, 1(1): 131-47.

The Indian Perspective of Spirituality. *ICPR Newsletter* (April–September 2011): 5-8.

Yoga-Advaita Psychology: An Inclusive Psychology of the Future. In A.K. Chowhan and S.S. Nathewat (eds). *New Facets of Positivism* (pp. 111-40). New Delhi: Macmillan.

2012

Bapu and Anna (Editorial). *GITAM Journal of Gandhian Studies*, 1(1): 1-3.

Complimentarity of Advaita Non-dualism and Yoga Dualism in Indian Psychology. *Journal of Consciousness Studies*, 19(9-10): 121-42.

Indian Psychology Curriculum: Moving beyond Borrowed Knowledge. In C. Alvares and S.S. Faruqi (eds), *Decolonizing the University: The Emerging Quest for Non-Eurocentric Paradigms* (pp. 255-66). Pulan Pinang: Penerbit Universiti Sains Malaysia.

Indian Psychology and Positive Psychology. Presidential Address. Seminar on Spirituality and Positive Psychology, 29 September 2012. Kolkata: Ramakrishna Mission Institute of Culture.

Marx and the Mahatma (Editorial). *GITAM Journal of Gandhian Studies*, 1(2): 265-76.

Parapsychology and Yoga: Theory and Practice. In S. Kakar and J.J. Kripal (eds), *Seriously Strange: Thinking about Psychic Experiences* (pp. 174-208). New Delhi: Penguin/Viking.

Psychology in the Indian Tradition. Invited address given at XXXth International Congress of Psychology 2012, Cape Town, South Africa. *Psychological Studies*, 15 (October 2012): 323-30.

Spiritual Reconstruction in Philosophy: The Vedantic Way. In G.N. Jha, B.R. Singh, R.P. Singh, and D. Mishra (eds), *Modern Perspectives on Vedanta: Proceedings of the 20th International Congress of Vedanta* (pp. 55-83). New Delhi: DK Printworld.

Violence and Nonviolence in Gandhi's Philosophy of Life. *GITAM Journal of Gandhian Studies*, 1(1): 131-48.

Gandhi's Touch: Spiritualizing Socialism. *ICPR Newsletter* (Jan.–April 2012): 2-7.

2013

Foreword. In B. Gopala Reddy (P. Adeswara Rao, tr.), *She Series*. Visakhapatnam: Loknayak Foundation.

Foreword. In G. Misra, *Psychology and Psychoanalysis,* pp. xix-xxii. New Delhi: Centre for Studies of Civilizations.

Consciousness and Yoga Psychology. In K.R. Rajani (ed.), *Mind and Consciousness: Some Contemporary Perspectives* (pp. 1-26). New Delhi: Akanksha Publishing House.

Indian Psychology. Its Many-sided Splendor. In A. Choudry and V.K. Vinayachandra (eds), *Perspectives on Indian Psychology* (pp. 36-37). Bangalore: Jain University Press.

Positive Psychology from the Perspective of Indian Psychology. In N. Sanyal (ed.), *Spirituality and Positive Psychology* (pp. 42-90). Kolkata: Ramakrishna Mission Institute of Culture.

Indian Psychology: Implications and Application. In R.M.M. Cornelissen, G. Misra, and S. Varma (eds), *Foundations and Applications of Indian Psychology* (pp. 3-17). Delhi: Pearson.

Indian Psychology, Parapsychology and Spiritual Psychology.

International Journal of Yoga, Philosophy and Parapsychology, I (January–June 2013): 4-14.

Gandhi and Economics. *GITAM Journal of Gandhian Studies*, 2(1): 117-34.

Spiritual Psychology, Indian Psychology and Parapsychology. Keynote Address in National Seminar on Spiritual Psychology, 23 March, Aligarh Muslim University.

Model of the Person in Indian Psychology. Presentation in The Twentieth Conference on Towards a Science of Consciousness, TSC–2013, 5 March, Agra: Dayalbagh Educational Institute.

2014

Foreword. In J.P. Das, *Consciousness Quest: Where East Meets West*, pp. ix-xiii New Delhi: Sage Publications.

Positive Psychology and Indian Psychology in Need of Reinforcement. *Psychological Studies*, 59(2): 94-102.

Gandhi's Darśana: A Philosophical Framework for Gandhi's Ideas and Practices. *GITAM Journal of Gandhian Studies*, 3(2): 333-62.

Dialectics of Gandhian Economics. Valedictory Address, 95th Indian Economic Association Annual Conference, 29 December 2013.

Gandhian Dialectics of Human Development. *Journal of Indian Psychology*, 28(1-2): 5-25.

Indian Psychology in Prospect. *Psychological Studies*, 59(2): 124-34.

Satyāgraha: Gandhi's Yoga of Nonviolence. *GITAM Journal of Gandhian Studies*, 3(1): 79-118.

Dialectical Spirituality: A Philosophical Framework for Gandhi's Thought and Practices. National seminar on Gandhi on Peace: Social Harmony and Conflict Resolution, Bodh-Gaya: Central University of Bihar.

Gandhi's Dharma. Invited Address, the Second International Conference on Dharma-Dhamma, Bhopal: Sanchi University.

Gandhian Dialectics of Human Development. National seminar on Where Do We Go from Here in Indian Psychology?". Visakhapatnam: GITAM University.

Curved Contours and Twisted Growth of Higher Education in Third World Countries. Keynote Address in International Conference on Rejuvenating Universities in Developing Countries: Challenges and Prospects, 19-20 December. Visakhapatnam: GITAM University.

2015

Towards Understanding Satyāgraha and How It Works. Keynote Address at National Seminar on Peace and Conflict Resolution: Gandhian Perspective.

Synthesis of Yoga and Advaita in the Gandhian Dialectic: Some Psycho-social Implications. Paper uploaded in Academia. edu.

Mahatma Gandhi on Human Nature: Implications for Human Development. Keynote Address at National Conference on Human Development and Family Studies: Crystalizing Disciplinary Identity in India, 17 October.

Indianization of Health Psychology: A Plea for Reorienting Psychological Practices in India Lecture at Department of Health Psychology, 6 August, Hyderabad, AP: University of Hyderabad.

Mahatma Gandhi: A Case Study of Excellence in Indian Tradition. Keynote Address in 3rd World Congress of Excellence, 19 October 2015. Chandigarh: Panjab University.

Indian Psychology: A Case Study of Mahatma Gandhi. Keynote Address in Centenary Conference, Centenary Psychology, 8-10 October 2015, Kolkata.

2016

Perpetual Peace: A Philosopher's Pipe Dream? Presidential Address in Second Asian Philosophy Congress. Visakhapatnam: GITAM University.

Internationalizing the Teaching of Consciousness with Grant

J. Rich. In G. J. Rich, U. Gielen, and H. Takooshian (eds), *Internationalizing the Teaching of Psychology* (pp. 297-311). Charlotte, NC: Information Age Publishing.

Meditation: Mindless and Mindful – Discovering the Human and Realizing Peace and Harmony. Keynote Address in International Conference on Being Human in Multicultural Traditions, March 2016. Visakhapatnam: Andhra University.

Indian Psychology: A Paradigm for Psychological Study of Spirituality with Anand C. Paranjpe. American Psychological Association.

Andhra University: My Academic Mother. Outline Speech delivered at Andhra University, 14 December 2016, Visakhapatnam.

2017

Mahatma Gandhi's Pragmatic Spirituality: Its Relevance to Psychology East and West. Psychological Studies, April, pp. 1-8.

Foreword. In K.R. Rajini and Bhaskar Vyas's *Contemporizing Raj Yoga: Neuroscience and Practices*. New Delhi: Concept Publishing Company.

Perpetual Peace: A Philosopher's Pipe Dream, *GITAM Journal of Gandhian Studies*, 5(2): 457-77.

Peace and War. Address given at Eighth Convocation of GITAM University, Hyderabad on 18 November 2017.

Gandhi: An Organizational Guru – In Pursuit of Peace. *GITAM Journal of Gandhian Studies*, 6(1-2): 119-30.

2018

On the Nature of Mind. In Girishwar Mishra's *Psychology: Explorations into Psyche and Psychology: Some Emerging Perspectives*, vol. 5 (pp. 1-91). New Delhi: Oxford University Press.

Ahimsa: The Mantra to Save Humankind from Self-Destruction. Address given at Ninth Convocation of GITAM University, Visakhapatnam on 15 September 2018.

Exploring Inner Space. Address given at Ninth Convocation of GITAM University, Hyderabad on 22 September 2018.

2019

Gandhi: An Organizational Guru. Address given at Tenth Convocation of GITAM University in Bengaluru on 2 November 2019.

Gandhi on Peace Social Harmony and Conflict Resolution. Address given at Tenth Convocation of GITAM University in Visakhapatnam on 9 November 2019.

M.K. Gandhi: An Epitome of Excellence in Indian Tradition. Address given at Tenth Convocation of GITAM University in Hyderabad on 15 November 2019.

Reviews and Assessment

K.R. Rao: A Profile by B. Sambasiva Prasad. 2016. In *Ageless Mind and Timeless Ideas,* ed. V. Balamohan Das and K.R. Rajini. New Delhi: D.K. Printworld.

K.R. Rao's Academic Journey of Sixty Plus Years by V. Gowri Rammohan. 2016. In *Ageless Mind and Timeless Ideas,* ed. V. Balamohan Das and K.R. Rajini. New Delhi: D.K. Printworld.

Reflections on the Man & His Mind: A Festschrift on the 85th Birthday of Koneru Ramakrishna Rao, ed. B. Nalini and Rosetta Joseph. 2017. New Delhi: D.K. Printworld.